Essentials of Person-Environment-Correspondence Counseling

Essentials of Person-Environment-Correspondence Counseling

Lloyd H. Lofquist
and
René V. Dawis

University of Minnesota Press
Minneapolis   Oxford

Published by the University of Minnesota Press
2037 University Avenue Southeast, Minneapolis, MN 55414
Printed in the United States of America on acid-free paper

Library of Congress Cataloging-in-Publication Data

Lofquist, Lloyd H.
    Essentials of person-environment-correspondence counseling /
Lloyd H. Lofquist and René V. Dawis.
        p.   cm.
    Includes bibliographical references and index.
    ISBN 0-8166-1889-5
    1. Counseling.   2. Environmental psychology.   I. Dawis,
René V.   II. Title.   III. Title: Person-environment-
    correspondence counseling.
    BF637.C6L65   1991
    158'.3—dc20   90-25916
                                                                CIP

A CIP catalog record for this book is available from the British
Library

The University of Minnesota is an
equal-opportunity educator and employer.

To our wives
Lillian Lofquist
and
Lydia Dawis

Contents

Preface   ix

Chapter 1.   Introduction   1

Chapter 2.   The Need for Theory in Counseling   5

Chapter 3.   Central Concepts of the P-E-C Theory   13

Chapter 4.   Formal Statement of the P-E-C Theory   29

Chapter 5.   Developmental Antecedents of Concepts
in the P-E-C Theory   39

Chapter 6.   The Counseling Process   46

Chapter 7.   The Self-Image in P-E-C Theory   62

Chapter 8.   Assessment in Counseling   74

Chapter 9.   Applying the P-E-C Theory of Counseling   86

Chapter 10. Postscript   107

Appendix   109

References   165

Index   169

Preface

The influence of our mentor, Professor Donald G. Paterson, shaped the direction of our research and our commitment to the science of psychology and its application to counseling psychology. The Paterson heritage requires dedication to what has been called the Minnesota Point of View. In earlier years, and with reference to the disastrous national drought of the 1930s, Minnesota applied psychology, with its strong emphases on research and measurement, was referred to as Dustbowl Empiricism. The term was used in a denigrating way, but Minnesotans rather liked it. They were independent and steadfast in their dedication to empirical research.

The Minnesota Point of View, which still characterizes Minnesota applied psychology, may be briefly summarized as follows: concepts should be defined; definitions should be operational so that they can be measured; questions should be approached through empirical research; the measurement of individual differences is central; conclusions should be based on objective data rather than on subjective surmise; and research should focus on the search for results that can be applied. The watchwords of the Minnesota Point of View are *definition, measurement, research, data, prediction,* and *application.* This is the context in which the Person-Environment-Correspondence (P-E-C) Theory of Counseling was developed.

Counseling psychology has moved over the years from its emphases on career choice and guidance, through career counseling, vocational development, and adjustment to work, to a much broader set of practices designed to address many kinds of adjustment problems. The counseling program at Minnesota has continued to explore in depth the problems and practices that fall generally in the area of adjustment to work. The findings and technology derived from many years of extensive research in this area can now, through the P-E-C Theory, be generalized and applied to the broad range of problems dealt with by counseling psychologists in work and nonwork environments.

It is our hope that this articulation of the theory will provide a useful framework for the teaching and practice of counseling and will stimulate additional research.

We wish to acknowledge the continuing significant contributions of our colleague Professor David J. Weiss to our work-adjustment research and to the development of instruments necessary to operationalize work-adjustment theory and the theory presented in this book. We are also grateful to Betty Adams for her many contributions to the operation of the counseling program, the Vocational Assessment Clinic, and our research groups. Special thanks are due Diane Krause, for typing the manuscript and for being patient with us about editorial changes along the way. Over the years we have been fortunate in having high-quality graduate student research assistants who have been delightful as co-workers, contributors, and critics.

Lloyd Lofquist
René Dawis

Chapter 1

Introduction

The Person-Environment-Correspondence (P-E-C) Theory of Counseling is based on the idea that most problems brought to counselors by clients stem from lack of fit, or discorrespondences, between the person and the environment. We believe that many problems presented by clients, however they are characterized, have their roots in discorrespondence between the clients and those environments that figure prominently in their lives. We have written the theory to provide interested counselors with a framework for practice and research. We have drawn liberally on the concepts of the Theory of Work Adjustment, developed through research and practice over the last thirty years, but the P-E-C Theory goes beyond the adjustment to work to address the whole gamut of problems presented to counselors. We describe the theory in the paragraphs that follow, to provide a context for the later formalization of the theory in more detailed and systematic terms.

Individuals are intrinsically motivated to achieve and maintain an optimal balance in their relationships with their environments. In their development from birth to physical maturity, they develop capabilities for responding to environmental requirements and preferences for the stimulus conditions for responding. Individuals seek to replicate in a given environment the positive reinforcing stimulus conditions they have experienced and to avoid negative experiences. Correspondence with an environment is indicated by the individual's satisfaction with the environmental reinforcement; the individual experiences positive reinforcement as a pleasant affective state. If the person is to remain in such an environment, he or she must perform satisfactorily. The individual's preferences for stimulus conditions are called *psychological needs,* and they may be viewed as the individual's requirements of the environment. Abilities and psychological needs stabilize for most individuals by the time they reach physical maturity, and they may be measured reliably. Individuals differ, environments differ, and each individual-environment interaction is unique.

Clients typically express the problems they are experiencing in terms other than individual-environment discorrespondence, or lack of fit. Such expressions reflect feelings of current dissatisfaction and are often referred to in learned, socially acceptable ways, as, for example, anxiety, stress, worry, or burnout. The roots of the problems may be found in the analysis of client-environment discorrespondence.

Clients respond in a number of environments, such as family, social activities, and work. The counselor and the client can together establish hierarchies of environmental salience for the client, determining which environments figure most prominently in the client's life. One hierarchy may be based on the number and intensity of the problems the client is having in responding; another may be based on the importance of the environments for facilitating the client's self-realization. By comparing ratings and discussing the environments, the counselor and client should arrive at a decision concerning the environment(s) on which to focus the P-E-C counseling.

The client's personality characteristics (abilities and psychological needs) and the characteristics of the target environment can be analyzed for goodness of fit, noting significant correspondences and discorrespondences. The counselor can teach the client how to use adjustment modes that focus on changing the environment, self, or both. In the process of looking at and trying to enhance person-environment correspondence, it is important to consider both objective fit, based on measurements, and subjective fit, based on client perceptions. With some clients it may be necessary to work on improving perceptual accuracy.

Client satisfaction with counseling should increase with a decrease in the number of discorrespondences the client perceives with the target environment(s). Satisfactory counseling should result in fewer and less intense problem behaviors as judged through observation of the client's cognitive, affective, and motor behaviors. This should bring the client's concerns about the original presenting problem within tolerable limits.

From their experiences with positive and negative reinforcers as a consequence of responding in many environments, individuals develop a set of preferences at various strengths for responding in certain stimulus conditions (preferences for certain reinforcers). These preferences become relatively stable at physical maturity and can be assessed for an individual. We call them psychological needs, or we sometimes refer to the values that underlie them. Each individual, then, has a set of psychological needs that he or she seeks to satisfy to achieve correspondence with an environment. Individuals seek to replicate in an environment the positive conditions they have experienced in their response and reinforcement history and to avoid negative experiences. Psychological needs may be thought of as an individual's requirements of an environment. They constitute one major set of dimensions in the individual's personality. The other major set of dimensions consists of the abilities the individual has developed over the same response and reinforcement history that make it possible for the person to respond to the requirements of an environment.

In applying the concepts of this theory, it is extremely important to be aware of individual differences. Individuals differ in the major dimensions of their personalities, and environments differ in the reinforcers they provide and the tasks they require. Each individual-environment interaction is unique and is characteristic of a particular client. Although the counselor may use the same procedures and interventions with different clients, the ways in which these are applied should be tailored for each individual client even if the presenting problems are stated in the same way.

The counselor takes the following steps in P-E-C counseling:

establishes an accepting and participatory relationship with the client

gathers information on which environments are most important to the client determines how the client and the important environments interact with each other

assesses both the individual and the target environment(s) on the main sets of dimensions in the interaction (needs-abilities and reinforcers and requirements, respectively)

establishes with the client the objective (data-based) fit (correspondence) and the subjective (client-perceived) fit

explores with the client additional information about the interaction and the client's reactions

considers with the client the adjustive modes that might be applied, such as acting on the environment or self to redress discorrespondence to achieve a better fit

assigns client homework, such as trying out adjustment action(s) or gaining additional information

slowly, but with progressively stronger emphasis over the series of interviews, discusses with the client the likely relationship of the person-environment discorrespondence (and its redress) to the original presenting problem

Chapter 2
The Need for Theory in Counseling

Since the beginning of this century, professional counseling has been offered as a response to the need of individuals to adjust to situations that arise in a variety of contexts. Problems arise in environments such as work, family, school, community, and interpersonal settings. Individuals react in different ways to similar circumstances. The same objective situation may be perceived by some as a problem that requires adjustment and by others as no problem at all. Even individuals in the same family may respond in quite different ways to the same problem situations. It is a truism that people differ, environments differ, perceptions of problems differ, and modes of adjustment differ.

Individual differences are an inescapable fact, and the ways in which people differ can be complex. On almost any human attribute normal people will differ, and their differences will be distributed around an average or typical person. Examples of these individual differences are described in texts such as those by Anastasi (1958), Minton and Schneider (1980), Tyler (1965), and Willerman (1979). These books describe individual differences in psychological attributes that are measured in metric terms—that is, numerical values. Williams (1956) has described individual differences in biological attributes, some of which are dramatic and run against our usual ways of thinking. For example, there is a distribution of temperatures for normal people; 98.6° F is simply the average. Also, there are many different sizes and shapes of body organs (e.g., hearts and livers) in normally functioning people. There are, in fact, "distributions" of normal hearts and livers, the averages being similar to typical textbook illustrations.

The complexity of the individuality that arises from individual differences can be illustrated by considering combinations of differences on simple dimensions such as height and weight. We typically expect taller persons to weigh more and shorter persons to weigh less. However, we all know some individuals who are tall but light in weight and others who are short and heavy. One may complicate this further by adding differences in other attributes. For example, short and heavy people may be fast or slow, bright or dull, dexterous or clumsy, strong or weak, and so on.

Environments also differ in a number of characteristics. At the simplest levels, they can be described as different in such terms as clean or dirty, quiet or noisy, spacious or crowded, bright or dark, and warm or cold. At more complex levels they may be described as tense or relaxed, predictable or unpredictable, and flexible or rigid. These examples should serve to illustrate the individual nature and complexity of environments to which individuals must adjust. Some people and environments are compatible, whereas other combinations can create problem situations.

In our society many environments are constructed by humans with only the typical person in mind. When this is the case, problems will arise because the environments cannot accommodate the individual differences in the persons who will be placed in them. We have, then, individually different people placed in individually different environments who are constrained by the lack of accommodation of environments constructed on the model of the typical or average person.

Any counseling theory must attend to individual differences and allow for their expression. Many approaches to professional counseling focus on the general applicability of a theory, school of thought, or set of techniques for use with all individuals and, in some instances, all problems as well. These approaches neglect the very important fact of individual differences. In this book, the emphasis will be on an approach that focuses strongly on individual differences and entails individualized counseling.

The theory presented in this book arises from our own need to draw upon and, we hope, integrate many of the important contributions of a diverse group of other counseling theorists and contributors to knowledge and technique in counseling. Most of these contributors focused mainly on vocational psychology, career development, career choice, and adjustment to work. Some have focused on psychotherapy and counseling. Over the last forty years counseling psychology has moved away from an exclusive focus on problems of vocational adjustment to a broader base that includes psychotherapy and dealing with problems that arise in nonwork environments. The P-E-C Theory of Counseling is designed to address a broad base of problems and is somewhat eclectic in that its concepts reflect some ideas similar to those of other theorists. The following paragraphs briefly describe some of these similarities.

Sigmund Freud's (1943) pleasure principle (that is, that individuals seek to avoid pain and to achieve gratification) can be seen as avoiding aversive stimuli, seeking positive reinforcement, and experiencing the resulting pleasurable affective state (i.e., satisfaction). When the pleasure principle is paired with the reality principle (the requirements and demands of the external world), one can assume the need to strive (be motivated) for person-environment fit, or correspondence with the external world (the environment). A major difference, of course, is that Freud refers to "instinctive" urges, whereas the P-E-C theory specifies psychological needs derived as high-strength preferences during a reinforcement history of responding in a variety of environments. Freud's *homeostasis* could be paraphrased as maintaining perceived correspondence (constancy). This perception of constancy or correspondence may be thought of as an appraisal of how well environmental (reality) conditions permit the expression of internal needs (urges). To address this question it seems reasonable to assume that the therapist and client need to engage in intensive analysis of environments as well as in thorough analysis of the individual.

On a quite different plane, **Frank Parsons** (1909), the founder of vocational guidance, focused on problems related to the choice of careers.

His formula—self-analysis plus job analysis plus reasoning equals wise vocational choice—clearly described an approach to person-environment correspondence theory as the framework for practice that would achieve work adjustment, finding pleasure in work (satisfaction) and being able to do the job (satisfactoriness). As Donald G. Paterson has said, Parsons had a workable formula and the right goals, but when he sought tools for individual and environment assessment he found the "cupboard was bare" and had to limit himself in practice to interviewing, client report, and some knowledge and some stereotypes of occupational characteristics, with a touch of the still-lingering pseudoscience of phrenology thrown in. His work was classic, but the technology he needed had not been developed.

Donald G. Paterson (1930) vigorously set out to "lay [to rest] the ghosts of pseudopsychology," to promote knowledge of and attention to individual differences, and he espoused a matching model for use in vocational guidance and in addressing problems related to work. He and his Minnesota colleagues developed many assessment instruments to measure the individual side of his person-environment fit model. Paterson did not propose a theory, but his commitment to a correspondence model is illustrated by his development, with Gerken and Hahn (1953), of the Minnesota Occupational Rating Scales. These scales were designed to facilitate a match of measured characteristics of individuals with rated descriptions of occupational categories. Measured occupational characteristics were not yet available to Paterson and his colleagues.

Morris Viteles (1932) provided significant foundation work for the Paterson type of approach and the development of vocational guidance and industrial psychology. He developed the job psychograph, using expert ratings to describe vocational-environment characteristics in person terms for application in counseling and personnel selection.

Anne Roe (1956) described fields and levels of work using assessment data on individuals obtained from the broad psychology literature. A commitment to person-environment fit is implicit in her resulting taxonomy of the world of work. Roe's description of the importance and effects of early experiences on the shaping of personality characteristics and preferences is also of interest to us. This work can be thought of as contributing to that part of the P-E-C Theory of Counseling that describes the role of environmental experiences with responding that is in turn described as the individual's reinforcement history. Rounds, Dawis, and Lofquist (1979) have demonstrated the importance of biographical (experience) information as it relates to psychological needs as they are viewed in this theory.

One could think of **Albert Ellis's** (1962) approach in Rational Emotive Therapy as basically working to correct distortions, misperceptions, or skewed subjective appraisals of the kind and amount of correspondence necessary between self and the objective world. A major counselor task in the P-E-C Theory approach might well be to facilitate the unclouding of the subjective evaluation of correspondence by seeking to eliminate the "musts" or "shoulds" by helping the client to learn the objective (measured) state of the correspondence. Perhaps then the subjective evaluation might be corrected to approach a point of consonance with the objective assessment of the individual-environment correspondence.

Carl Rogers (1951) contributed an important focus on the client's perception of self and on ways of facilitating the growth of the client to the point of developing an organized conceptualization of his or her self characteristics and their relationship to others and to the various aspects of life. We feel it logical to extend Rogers's ideas well beyond the "within client" therapy situation and the facilitation of self-development to equal concentration on environmental consequences experienced with actual external behavior and the resulting client perceptions of congruence (correspondence), that is, self-experiences being accurately symbolized in the self-concept, or incongruence between self and experience (which will require adjustment). It would also seem reasonable to assume that an organized conceptualization of self would be heavily dependent for content on the pattern and levels of the client's psychological needs. It may well be that tension, uneasiness, and anxiety may stem from either or both the lack of an adequately formulated and understood self-concept or the perception of discorrespondence when the self is tested against environmental reality factors. Problem solving and improved adjustment may require not only client knowledge of self but also knowledge of the kinds of environmental characteristics against which the self may be actualized with positive affective consequences (i.e., environmental characteristics that are congruent or correspondent with self and yield satisfaction).

B. F. Skinner's (1938) operant conditioning and discovery of contingencies and schedules of reinforcement (stimuli following behavioral responses) and their differential effects on learning provide the background for our conceptualization of reinforcement histories and the development (learning) of patterns and levels of psychological needs (preferences at some level of strength for responding in certain stimulus conditions). Biographical information that describes reinforcement history can be used to forecast psychological needs, which, in turn, when addressed by correspondent stimulus conditions in the environment, permit the prediction of satisfaction by the individual. In addition, the use of reinforcement techniques in the counseling process contributes a great deal to the counselor's intervention skills in Person-Environment-Correspondence counseling.

Donald Super (1957) brought a developmental focus to vocational psychology and stimulated vocational psychologists to think about developmental issues such as vocational maturity, stages of developmental progress, and indicators of levels of vocational maturity. Influences from Super's work may be found in our conceptualization of an individual's response and reinforcement history and of the stages of development of the personality (i.e., the set of abilities, the set of needs, and the style dimensions). Stages of personality development are seen as moving from inception, through differentiation, to crystallization and stability as the response and reinforcement history develops across age spans to the point of physical maturity, when the typical individual manifests a differentiated and stable personality, from a measurement standpoint.

Super's (1962) development of the Work Values Inventory attests to his early advocacy of the importance of values to adjustment. There is similarity to be found in our strong emphasis on needs and values satisfaction as a major component of adjustment, and in our work on the development of the Minnesota Importance Questionnaire to measure psychological needs (see Rounds et al., 1981). Super's "values" and our "needs" and "values" were natural progressions from the earlier work by **Henry Murray** (1938) on the assessment of psychological needs.

E. K. Strong (1943) pointed out that the assessment of nonability vocational variables (specifically interests) is necessary for a more complete and richer conceptualization of vocational behavior. He demonstrated that vocational interests can be reliably and validly measured using an empirical approach. Strong, in the studies reported in his classic book *Vocational Interests 18 Years after College* (1955), established both the stability of interests and their utility in forecasting later occupational membership.

E. E. Ghiselli (1966) developed a taxonomy of occupations on the basis of ability requirements from an analysis of the validity coefficients of occupational aptitude tests. He also demonstrated significant relationships between abilities and satisfactoriness on the job. Studies like these lend support to the P-E-C approach to the prediction of satisfactoriness from the interaction of abilities and environmental ability requirements.

Beatrice Dvorak (1935), working with D. G. Paterson and his colleagues in the Minnesota Employment Stabilization Research Institute, did pioneering work that would later lead to the development of multifactor tests of abilities and to the publication of the General Aptitude Test Battery by the U.S. Department of Labor (1970). It then became feasible for counselors to assess several major abilities of an individual and to interpret results against a common norm group. Occupational Aptitude Patterns were then developed so that counselors could compare individuals' ability patterns to environmental requirements for similar abilities.

John Holland (1973), working with data on measured interests, developed a theory and practices for matching people and careers. His development of a system with six personality types and six parallel occupational modes to describe the occupations in the *Dictionary of Occupational Titles* (U.S. Department of Labor, 1977) has stimulated a great deal of research and wide use of his concepts and instruments in counseling.

The work of such research contributors as Paterson, Viteles, Dvorak, Super, Ghiselli, Strong, and Holland quite naturally provided both urgency and feasibility for the development of environmental taxonomies that describe both ability requirements and need reinforcers against which individuals' personalities can be compared for correspondence and the likelihood of adjustment. An example of such a taxonomy is provided by the Minnesota Occupational Classification System III (Dawis et al., 1987).

We have briefly mentioned only a few of the many individuals who have contributed significantly to theory and research in counseling. Those mentioned are the individuals whose work contributed most significantly to our thinking as we developed the Theory of Work Adjustment and the extension of its concepts in the development of the Person-Environment-Correspondence Theory of Counseling.

Chapter 3
Central Concepts of the P-E-C Theory

To provide a context for the formal statement of the Person-Environment-Correspondence Theory of Counseling, this chapter is devoted to defining concepts central to the theory and the terms used in it.

Personality

The P-E-C Theory of Counseling requires definition of the concept of personality in a way that specifies the principal components underlying the responding of individuals in environments. These components must be operationalized, assessed, and described in such ways that they may be compared to their counterparts in environments to permit analysis of the kinds and amounts of person-environment correspondence that exist in the person-environment interactions.

Personality, as we use the term here, is defined broadly as a complex of components that relate to individuals' capabilities for achieving satisfactoriness in environments, individuals' preferences for achieving satisfaction with environments, and individuals' styles of presenting capabilities and preferences to environments. It should be noted that this definition is much broader than what is measured by any one instrument typically referred to as a personality test.

Personality Structure

Personality structure is composed of two major sets of dimensions, abilities and needs. The expression of abilities, through the development of many specific skills, permits the demonstration of capabilities by an individual for use in meeting environmental requirements. A set of major ability dimensions is illustrated by the subtests of the General Aptitude Test Battery (GATB; U.S. Department of Labor, 1970) as follows:

G—general learning ability, the ability to understand underlying principles, to reason and make judgments

V—verbal ability, the ability to understand the meaning of words

N—numerical ability, the ability to perform arithmetic operations quickly and accurately and to reason numerically

S—spatial ability, the ability to grasp the two-dimensional representation of three-dimensional objects, and to think visually of geometric forms

P—form perception, the ability to see detail in shapes of objects, to make visual comparisons and discriminations in objects or pictures

Q—clerical ability, the ability to perceive detail in verbal and tabular material

K—eye-hand coordination, the ability to coordinate eyes with hands or fingers in making precise movements with speed

F—finger dexterity, the ability to manipulate small objects with the fingers rapidly and accurately

M—manual dexterity, the ability to move the hands easily and skillfully

The second major group of dimensions in the personality structure is a set of psychological needs, preferences for responding under specified stimulus conditions in an environment. A set of major psychological need dimensions is illustrated by the needs measured by the Minnesota Importance Questionnaire (MIQ; Rounds et al., 1981) as follows:

Ability Utilization—I could do something that makes use of my abilities.

Achievement—The job could give me a feeling of accomplishment.

Activity—I could be busy all the time.

Independence—I could work alone on the job.

Variety—I could do something different every day.

Compensation*—My pay would compare well with that of other workers.

Security—The job would provide for steady employment.

Working Conditions*—The job would have good working conditions.

Advancement—The job would provide an opportunity for advancement.

Recognition—I could receive recognition for the work I do.

Authority—I could tell people what to do.

Social Status—I could be "somebody" in the community.

Co-workers*—My co-workers would be easy to make friends with.

Moral Values—I could do the work without feeling that it is morally wrong.

Social Service—I could do things for other people.

Company Policies and Practices*—The company would administer its policies fairly.

Supervision-Human Relations*—My boss would back up the workers (with top management).

Supervision-Technical*—My boss would train the workers well.

Creativity—I could try out some of my own ideas.

Responsibility—I could make decisions on my own.

*Require adaptation to general (nonwork) environment characteristics.

Reference Dimensions

In the assessment and description of personality structure, abilities (underlying common elements of skills) and values (underlying common elements of needs) are used as reference dimensions for skills and needs, respectively. It is not feasible to assess and describe the very large numbers of skills extant across individuals and environments. Since skills derive from combinations of basic abilities, it is more reasonable to work with abilities as reference dimensions for skills. The kinds of abilities represented in the GATB are seen then as reference dimensions. In the interest of parsimony, the same kind of reasoning can be applied to the set of needs represented in the MIQ. The twenty MIQ needs can be described in terms of six values used as reference dimensions for needs as follows:

Achievement—the importance of an environment that encourages accomplishment

Comfort—the importance of an environment that is comfortable and not stressful

Status—the importance of an environment that provides recognition and prestige

Altruism—the importance of an environment that fosters harmony with and service to others

Safety—the importance of an environment that is predictable and stable

Autonomy—the importance of an environment that stimulates initiative

Personality Style

An additional component of personality describes basic ways in which individuals typically respond. It may be referred to as a set of personality-style dimensions. These dimensions are of importance since style of responding by individuals will affect the presentation of personality structure to environments. These personality-style variables may be illustrated as follows by the set of dimensions that have been presented by Dawis and Lofquist (1984):

Celerity—quickness of response in interacting with an environment

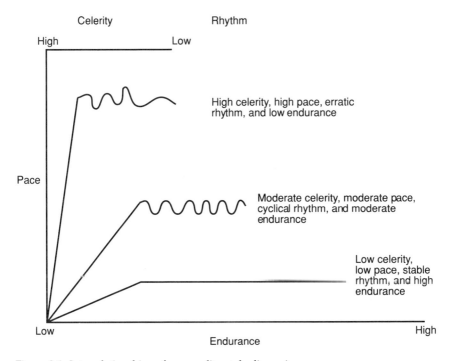

Figure 3.1. Interrelationships of personality-style dimensions

Pace—level of effort typically expended in interaction with an environment

Rhythm—pattern of pace

Endurance—likelihood of maintaining interaction with the environment

Figure 3.1 graphically shows the interrelationships among the personality-style dimensions.

Adjustment Style

In seeking to achieve and maintain correspondence with an environment, individuals will differ on a dimension of *flexibility*. Flexibility is defined as tolerance for discorrespondence with an environment before acting to reduce the discorrespondence. Individuals will also differ in the likelihood that they will employ one or both of two main modes of adjusting to discorrespondence. One mode is *activeness,* acting on the environment to change it to reduce discorrespondence. The other mode is *reactiveness,* acting on self to reduce discorrespondence. A fourth dimension of adjustment style is *perseverance,* which may be defined as persisting in adjustment behavior or continuing to tolerate discorrespondence with the environment as indicated by length of stay before leaving it. Figure 3.2 depicts the relationships among the adjustment-style dimensions.

Motivation

The impetus for individual-environment interaction comes from the fact the individuals inherently seek to achieve and to maintain correspondence with their environments. The level of this motivation will be affected by the individual's levels of flexibility, pace, and endurance, which, in turn, may be thought of as products of the individual's response and reinforcement history. Motivation as a personality dimension is a state variable rather than a trait variable and is probably less stable than the personality structure and style dimensions and can be influenced and enhanced through additional knowledge and more accurate perception learned in a counseling process.

Personality is conceptualized, then, in P-E-C Counseling Theory as a complex of components underlying individual responding in environments that may be described in terms of structure, style of responding, style of adjusting, and motivation.

Personality Development

The development of an individual's personality can be described by a history of response and reinforcement in many different stimulus conditions across several main environments. This reinforcement history produces the patterns (shapes and levels) of the personality structure

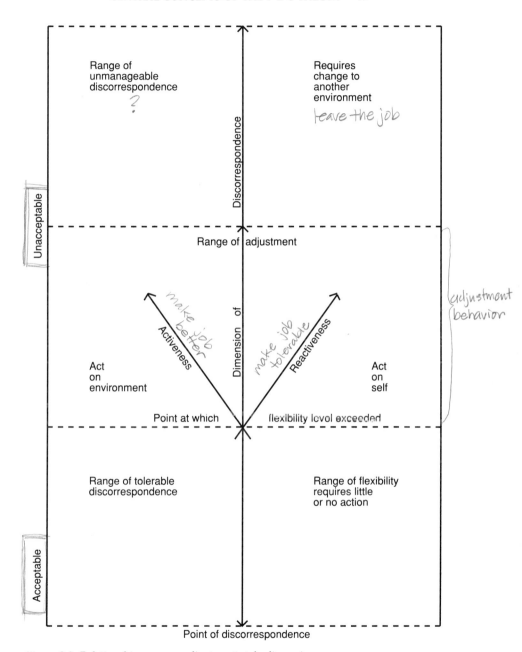

Figure 3.2. Relationships among adjustment-style dimensions

and style dimensions that the individual possesses at maturity. The individual progresses through three main stages of personality development:

Differentiation—period in which the the individual tries out, develops, and expands response capabilities and reinforcer preferences in terms of variety, range, and complexity

Stability—period characterized by the crystallization and maintenance of a response repertoire and a structure of reinforcer preference

Decline—period during which some response capabilities and some reinforcer preferences are affected by the aging process

The numbers, kinds, and levels of personality components that are crystallized and maintained by an individual are a function of both the hereditary potential of the individual for development and the richness of the individual's reinforcement history. A rich or full reinforcement history is one in which the individual has experienced a broad range of stimulus conditions for response over a normal variety of environmental settings. This kind of history and development is expected for most individuals. In some cases an impoverished reinforcement history (e.g., one resulting from a long history of institutionalization, overwhelming disability from birth, or severe socioeconomic disadvantage) may result in lack of crystallization of a clear and stable set of personality components.

Environment

For the analysis of person-environment correspondence it is necessary to describe environments in person terms that parallel the descriptors of personality and to use the same metrics. We can think of environments as having "personality." They contain ability requirements and provide reinforcers for needs to meet the individual's requirements. We can say, then, that they have personality structure. They have typical ways of responding, or personality style, and, when their flexibility level for tolerance of individual discorrespondence is exceeded, they employ adjustment styles to act on the individual for change or on themselves for change to enhance correspondence.

If the target for individual responding is the work environment, a considerable amount of technology is now available for use in describing the environment in the terms indicated above. For example, occupational aptitude (or ability) patterns (OAPs) are available and are expressed in GATB ability-requirement terms, occupational reinforcer patterns (ORPs) have been developed that describe reinforcer systems, and a taxonomy of work that integrates ability-requirement data and reinforcer-system data is available for use in making individual-environment comparisons for correspondence (Minnesota Occupational Classification System III, or MOCS III; Dawis et al., 1987).

For other main environments a good deal of research must still be done to provide an adequate technology. It is feasible, however, in these other environments to describe the environment "personality" by using interview data, observation, ratings, environment description questionnaires, and inferences from past behavior.

When working with P-E-C Theory where the individual's target is an environment where less-than-optimal technology is available, the search for necessary descriptive data will be on track if the concepts and principles of the theory are observed. As an example, if marriage is the environment, it is important to view each individual as having both response-capability requirements and reinforcer requirements of the other. Each individual has the personality components that have been described, and each serves as the environment "personality" for the other. For example, given adequate reciprocal response capabilities, one would not simply assume correspondence and adjustment if the needs of the two parties were similar. The more important question related to correspondence or discorrespondence in this environment would be whether or not each individual knew the psychological needs of the other and provided reinforcement for those needs.

As another example, it should be pointed out that a retirement environment may require levels of response capability in nonpaid volunteer activities, and these activities in turn have reinforcer systems for the satisfaction of psychological needs. Volunteer activities and combinations of retirement activities frequently have analogues in work environments, and it is possible to draw valid inferences from data that are available in a taxonomy of work such as MOCS III. Furthermore, inasmuch as MOCS III taxa are described in very generic terms for ability requirements and reinforcer characteristics, it should be possible to draw inferences for all general environments. To do this, one would have to estimate levels of generic ability requirements and reinforcer characteristics for the major activities of the environment.

Correspondence

Correspondence is the key concept in the P-E-C Theory of Counseling. It is what the individual is striving for in interactions with environments. It may be defined as the degree to which the requirements of either the individual or the environment are met by each other. Correspondence represents a harmonious relationship between the individual and the environment. It describes the suitability of the individual to the environment and of the environment for the individual. It may be thought of as consonance or agreement between the individual and the environment.

The dynamic interaction between the individual and the environment that takes place in achieving and maintaining correspondence is termed *corresponsiveness*. It is defined as a continuing reciprocal and complementary relationship between the individual and the environment. It is a relationship in which the individual and the environment are mutually responsive.

Formal statement of the P-E-C Theory and discussion of its applications require the use of several specific psychological terms. They are presented in alphabetical order and defined in the following section.

Terms Used in the P-E-C Theory of Counseling

Abilities—reference dimensions for skills

Abilities, mature—abilities that show stability on repeated measurement

Ability dimensions—basic dimensions that represent common elements of skill dimensions; reference dimensions for the description of skills

Ability pattern—description of an individual in terms of relative levels of different abilities

Ability requirement pattern—description of an environment in terms of the relative levels of different abilities required of an individual for adjustment

Ability tests—measures of ability dimensions

Activeness—reducing discorrespondence by acting to change the environment; acting on the environment to increase correspondence

Adjustment—achievement and maintenance of correspondence with an environment resulting in satisfactoriness and satisfaction

Adjustment indicators—individual satisfaction, the individual's satisfactoriness, and length of time an individual remains in an environment

Adjustment mode—approach used by an individual to reduce discorrespondence or increase correspondence; description of individual adjustment behavior in terms of activeness or reactiveness

Adjustment style—description of an individual on personality dimensions of flexibility, activeness, reactiveness, and perseverance

Behavior development, decline stage—period in which some response capabilities and reinforcer preferences are affected by the aging process

Behavior development, differentiation stage—period in which the individual is observed to try out, develop, and expand response capabilities and reinforcer preferences in terms of their variety, range, and complexity

Behavior development, stability stage—period characterized by the crystallization and maintenance of a response repertoire and a structure of reinforcer preferences

Celerity—quickness of response in interacting with an environment

Correspondence—degree to which the requirements of either the individual or the environment are met by each other; harmonious relationship between the individual and the environment; suitability of the individual to the environment and of the environment for the individual; consonance or agreement between the individual and the environment

Corresponsiveness—continuing reciprocal and complementary relationship between the individual and the environment; relationship in which the individual and the environment are corresponsive (i.e., mutually responsive)

Endurance—likelihood of maintaining interaction with the environment

Flexibility—tolerance for discorrespondence with the environment before acting to reduce the discorrespondence

Individual differences—differences among people on any given behavioral dimension; differences in an individual's standing in a group from one behavioral dimension to another; differences in an individual's standing on a given behavioral dimension from one time to another; combinations of the above

Interests—preferences (liking or disliking) for various kinds of activities, resulting from the interaction of abilities and needs

Interests, exhibited—preferences for activities inferred from observations of an individual's participation in activities or from records of such participation

Interests, expressed or stated—preferences for activities as stated by an individual

Interests, latent—interests that appear much later than usual (i.e., well after physical maturity)

Interests, measured—preferences for activities as expressed by an individual on a structured, standardized psychometric instrument designed to sample a broad domain of activities

Interests, validated—preferences for activities established from agreement among expressed or stated, measured, and exhibited interests

Interests, vicarious—interests that are based on someone else's experience

Main general environments—broad environmental classes that encompass several behaviors of an individual that are similar in their direction toward achieving adjustment in each one of the overall environmental classes (e.g., educational, family, home, retirement, social, and work)

Need reinforcers—classes of stimulus conditions the presence or absence of which is associated with the satisfaction of needs

Needs—an individual's requirements for reinforcers at given levels of reinforcement strength; an individual's preferences for stimulus conditions experienced to have been reinforcing

Pace—level of effort typically expended in interaction with an environment

Perseverance—persistence in adjustment activity; tolerance of discorrespondence with the environment as indicated by length of stay before leaving it; length of time an individual seeks to reduce intolerable discorrespondence

Personality description, exhibited—description of an individual's personality based on direct observation or on records of observers

Personality description, expressed or stated—self-reported description of an individual's personality in terms of the likelihood of behaving in particular ways

Personality description, measured—description of an individual's personality made within the framework of a psychometric instrument constructed to sample and scale a broad range of human behaviors in systematic fashion

Personality description, validated—description of personality based on the agreement of exhibited and measured personality descriptions

Personality structure—status characteristics of the personality; skills and needs; abilities and values as reference dimensions for skills and needs; the individual's set of abilities, set of values, and the relationships among and between these abilities and values

Personality structure, crystallization of—retention of a particular set of abilities and values in the personality structure

Personality structure, inception of—initial development of abilities and values

Personality structure, individuation of—process of crystallization and stabilization of abilities and values

Personality structure, stabilization of—maintenance of abilities and values at relatively constant levels of strength and hierarchical ordering

Personality style—process characteristics of the personality; the individual's typical ways of interacting with the environment; description of the individual on dimensions of celerity, pace, rhythm, and endurance; description of how an individual utilizes abilities in the context of values in terms of quickness or slowness of responding, level of activity, pattern of activity, and length of responding

Presenting problem—Individual's description of problem for which counseling assistance is sought, typically broad and presented in learned and socially acceptable terms

Psychological needs—requirements for reinforcers at particular strengths regardless of their derivation, measured as self-reported requirements or as observed requirements

Reactiveness—reducing discorrespondence by acting on self to change expression of personality structure; changing the expression or manifestation of personality structure to increase correspondence

Reinforcement—process of providing reinforcers that maintain or increase response rate

Reinforcement strength—frequency level of responding associated with a given reinforcer; frequency level of responding that is experienced (actual), reported by an individual (stated), or reported by an observer (observed)

Reinforcer factors—reference dimensions for the description of reinforcers

Reinforcer pattern—description of an environment in terms of the relative presence or absence of different kinds of reinforcers

Reinforcers—stimulus conditions observed to be consistently associated with increased rate of response over the base rate; stimulus conditions that are associated with the maintenance of response and the likelihood of future response

Responses—reactions to the environment or actions on the environment

Rewards—stimulus conditions intended to serve as effective reinforcers

Rhythm—typical pattern of pace

Salient problem environment—the main general environment indicated by the client's ratings and by counselor inferences from client behaviors to contain the highest number or the greatest intensity of adjustment problems

Salient importance environment—the main general environment rated by the client to be the most important for the realization of the client's self-image, that is, for ideal adjustment

Satisfaction—an individual's positive affective evaluation of the target environment; result of an individual's requirements being fulfilled by the target environment; internal indicator of correspondence; a pleasant affective state; the individual's appraisal of the extent to which his or her requirements are fulfilled by the environment

Satisfactoriness—satisfaction of the environment with the individual; result of an individual fulfilling the requirements of the environment; external indicator of correspondence; work environment's appraisal of the extent to which its requirements are fulfilled by the individual

Self-image—the individual's organized conceptual set of perceived characteristics of self and of the relationship of self to others and to environments

Skill dimension—common skill identified for several individuals, defined in terms of level of difficulty, economy of effort, and efficiency

Skills—recurring response sequences that become more refined with repetition; behaviors requiring exercise or use of several different abilities in combination

Social norms—standards of behavior that have developed from the society's collective experience; prescriptions of socially acceptable behavior in a variety of environmental settings

Stable psychological needs—needs showing little change over successive measurements

Target environment—the main general environment determined by the client to be the focus for P-E-C counseling, following client-counselor analysis of the ratings of environmental-problem salience and importance salience

Value dimensions—basic importance dimensions that represent common elements in need dimensions; reference dimensions for the description of needs

Values—reference dimensions for needs

Chapter 4

Formal Statement of the P-E-C Theory

This chapter presents a formal statement of the P-E-C Theory of Counseling that integrates its central concepts and describes it in the terms defined in Chapter 3. It provides a framework against which to view supportive research findings and should generate hypotheses for future research that will lead to further explication of the theory.

Propositions and Corollaries of the Person-Environment-Correspondence Theory of Counseling

Proposition I: Individuals are inherently motivated to achieve and maintain optimal correspondence with their environments.

> *Corollary IA*: Individuals seek to replicate in an environment the positive (reinforcing) conditions experienced over their response and reinforcement history, i.e., those conditions with positive affective (satisfying) consequences.

> *Corollary IB*: Individuals seek to avoid negative (punishing) stimulus conditions experienced in an environment if they are experienced in their response and reinforcement history as having negative affective (dissatisfying) consequences.

> *Corollary IC*: Individuals experience both positive (satisfying) and negative (dissatisfying) affective consequences of their behavior in their response and reinforcement history.

> *Corollary ID*: Individuals' perceived levels of correspondence (or discorrespondence) are indicated by degree of satisfaction (or dissatisfaction).

> *Corollary IE*: Individuals require environments to meet reinforcer requirements to be judged as satisfying.

Proposition II: Individuals differ in response capabilities and reinforcer requirements; environments differ in response requirements and reinforcer capabilities.

Corollary IIA: Each total individual-environment interaction will be unique, but may have elements in common with other such interactions.

Corollary IIB: Individual adjustment requires an acceptable fit (correspondence), i.e., one that is satisfactory to the environment and satisfying to the individual.

Corollary IIC: Environments require individuals to demonstrate appropriate task performance to be judged satisfactory.

Corollary IID: Individual task performance depends on appropriate response capabilities.

Corollary IIE: Individuals require environments to supply appropriate reinforcers to be judged satisfying.

Corollary IIF: Environment satisfaction of individual needs depends on adequate reinforcer capabilities.

Corollary IIG: Satisfactoriness is necessary for the individual to continue to experience the reinforcing conditions of the environment.

Corollary IIH: Satisfaction is necessary for the individual to continue satisfactory task performance for the environment.

Proposition III: Individuals interact constantly with a variety of environments (e.g., educational, work, marital, familial, social), but some environments are more salient than others.

Corollary IIIA: Some environments are experienced for longer periods of time. Some environments have more emotional impact. Some are more intense; some more stressful. Such factors contribute to salience of the environment(s).

Proposition IV: Clients seek counseling when they are unable to meet their requirements for stimulus conditions in their environments that are satisfying.

Corollary IVA: Clients' inability to fulfill their requirements is frequently described in terms of different "presenting problems" to the counselor.

Corollary IVB: The roots of clients' presenting problems may be found in an analysis of the degree of client-environment discorrespondence.

Corollary IVC: Client-environment discorrespondence may be of two major types:

> a. client inability to meet environmental response requirements, and

> b. client inability to find environmental reinforcers to meet the client's reinforcer requirements.

Corollary IVD: Clients' expressions of presenting problems in terms other than individual-environment discorrespondence reflect learning to describe dissatisfaction in more habitual and socially accepted ways, such as in terms of "anxiety," "stress," or "burnout."

Proposition V: Counselors can deal with only some (not all) of the clients' environments. Salience of environments in terms of clients' necessity for achieving/maintaining correspondence will differ in amount.

> *Corollary VA*: Focusing on salient environments to redress discorrespondence is more feasible than attempting to deal with all the several environments in which the client behaves.

> *Corollary VB*: Some clients may require support (maintenance of client motivation) in the process of exploring their hierarchies of salient environments.

Proposition VI: Stimulus conditions that have been experienced by the client with positive or negative affective consequences can be assessed as preferences for some sets of stimulus conditions over others, i.e., as psychological needs.

> *Corollary VIA*: Client psychological needs can be assessed by inference in the interview by using biographical data, and by psychometric assessment.

Proposition VII: The presence or absence and level of stimulus conditions in environments can be assessed to describe their reinforcer systems.

> *Corollary VIIA*: Counselors can assess environmental reinforcer systems by observation, by eliciting client perceptions of the presence

or absence of reinforcers, or by generalizing from relevant research literature.

Proposition VIII: The effectiveness of the counseling relationship can be enhanced by knowledge of both client's and counselor's psychological needs.

Corollary VIIIA: Counselor behavior should attend to client expectations for reinforcement of psychological needs.

Corollary VIIIB: Counselors have "requirements" for client satisfaction of their (counselors') needs.

Proposition IX: Counselors have response requirements (goals) for clients.

Corollary IXA: Counselors can assess client capabilities from the client's history, from performance in the interview, and from psychometric assessment.

Corollary IXB: Counselor response requirements for clients should correspond with client response capabilities.

Proposition X: Clients have response requirements (expectations of results, outcomes) for counselors.

Corollary XA: Clients infer counselor response capabilities (expertness) from the training background, reputation, appearance, and behavior of the counselor, and from the professional setting in which the counselor operates.

Proposition XI: Satisfaction of psychological needs by stimulus conditions and satisfactory meeting of response requirements by response capabilities will be less than complete for both clients and counselors inasmuch as any counseling process will involve some compromise.

Corollary XIA: Counselor requirements should be subservient to client requirements.

Corollary XIB: Satisfaction of counselor psychological needs should be viewed as secondary to the satisfaction of client psychological needs.

Proposition XII: Counseling is a learning process that progresses from establishing a working relationship to assessing client requirements and characteristics of salient environments, evaluating person-environment correspondence, relating person-environment-correspondence data to presenting problem(s), determining and teaching adjustment strategies, and assessing the amount of resolution of the problem(s).

Proposition XIII: The amelioration or resolution of client problems requires that the client achieve adequate self-environment correspondence and accurate perception of this correspondence.

Corollary XIIIA: Clients' presenting problems arise from perceived self-environment discorrespondences in salient environments.

Corollary XIIIB: Resolution of presenting problems stemming from inaccurate perception of objectively correspondent P-E-C requires improving the accuracy of client perception.

Corollary XIIIC: Resolution of presenting problems stemming from accurate perception of objectively discorrespondent P-E-C requires reducing discorrespondence or changing environments to improve correspondence.

Corollary XIIID: Resolution of presenting problems stemming from inaccurate perception of objectively discorrespondent P-E-C as being correspondent requires intervention both to improve accuracy of perception and to redress the discorrespondence.

Proposition XIV: Client satisfaction with counseling is a function of decreases in client perception of discorrespondence.

Proposition XV: Satisfactoriness of counseling is indicated by decreases in the number and intensity of observable problem behaviors.

Proposition XVI: For counseling to be effective, decreases in client-perceived discorrespondences should be accompanied by decreases in the number and intensity of client problem behaviors.

Some Research Hypotheses

Following are some examples of research hypotheses that may be derived from the propositions and corollaries of the P-E-C Theory:

1. When an individual's reported experiences on a biodata form are used to construct a profile of inferred psychological needs, that profile will be highly similar to a psychological need profile generated from measured preferences for stimulus conditions (reinforcement), for example, by using an instrument such as the MIQ (Proposition VI).

2. Observers' (e.g., parents') recorded observations of an individual's experiences with reinforcing and aversive conditions during the development years will correlate positively with psychological needs reported as preferences by the individual when mature (Corollaries IA, IB, IC).

3. Individuals' ratings of the degree to which reinforcers in an environment meet their reinforcer requirements will be highly correlated with those individuals' global satisfaction with the environment (Corollaries ID, IE, IIE).

4. Individuals who have chosen environments with reinforcement patterns that meet their psychological needs will on follow-up express satisfaction with their environments, e.g., on a measure such as the MSQ (Corollary IE).

5. On the basis of measured abilities and measured psychological needs, individuals may be clustered into broader categories of communality of capabilities (such as perceptual, cognitive, motor) and value preferences (such as internal, social, environmental) at the same time that the members of the clusters are individually different in terms of their measured component abilities and needs (e.g., G, V, N for Cognitive; and ACH, AUT, STA for Internal) (Corollary IIA).

6. The same kind of clustering can be done for environmental capability requirements and reinforcer systems, for different environments, and for the person-environment interaction in which the two clustering systems may be used to show communalities in the P-E correspondence at the same time that the environments are individually different at the level of ability elements and value elements and degrees of P-E correspondence are unique at the component level (Corollary IIA).

7. Clients seeking counseling will express more dissatisfaction with their environments than persons from the same environments who do not seek counseling (Proposition IV).

8. The same kind of discorrespondence will be described by different individuals as different presenting problems (Corollaries IVA, IVD).

9. There is a correlation between kinds of discorrespondence and presenting problems that is positive but imperfect (Corollary IVA).

10. Reduction of discorrespondence through intervention should result in diminution of presenting problems, discorrespondence being measured as lack of person-environment fit and presenting problems in terms of number and intensity (Proposition XVI).

11. Past environments for which individuals express satisfaction will be similar, in terms of their salient reinforcer characteristics, to environments chosen later by the same individuals (Corollary IA).

12. Past environments for which individuals express dissatisfaction will be similar, in terms of their salient aversive characteristics, to later environments for which the same individuals express dissatisfaction (Corollary IB).

13. Past environments for which individuals were judged satisfactory will be similar, in terms of their salient response requirements, to later environments for which the same individuals will be judged satisfactory (Corollary IIC).

14. Past environments for which individuals were judged unsatisfactory will be similar, in terms of their salient response requirements, to later environments for which the same individuals will be judged unsatisfactory (Corollary IIC).

15. Client presenting problems arise from (a) inaccurate client perception of objectively correspondent P-E-C, (b) accurate client perception of objectively discorrespondent P-E-C, or (c) inaccurate client perception of objectively discorrespondent P-E-C (Corollary IVB).

16. Client accuracy of perception of P-E-C will be improved as the self-image becomes more correspondent to measured personality (i.e., behavior capability and reinforcer requirement) (Corollary XIIIB).

Research in Support of Basic P-E-C Concepts

This section contains a sampling of research that undergirds the basic concepts in the P-E-C Theory. Since the P-E-C Theory of Counseling is an extension of the model developed for the Theory of Work Adjustment (TWA) and rests heavily on TWA concepts, much of the research in support of TWA has relevance for the P-E-C Theory. Currently, some of the supportive research will be found in the publications of the Work Adjustment Project. Other support comes from the general research literature, particularly in industrial/organizational and counseling psychology. Premises and concepts underlying the P-E-C Theory will be stated and followed by brief statements of findings reached in particular research studies. The reader will wish to pursue the particular research references for more detail.

People differ. Individuals are unique in terms of their personality structure and style and their combination of physical characteristics.

The fact of individual differences across dimensions and traits is well documented in texts on individual differences such as those by Anastasi (1958) and Tyler (1965).

Williams (1956), in his book *Biochemical Individuality,* has demonstrated the facts of individual differences in biochemical and anatomical areas for normal individuals that a typical person would not think possible, such as in distributions of temperature, heart sizes and shapes, livers, and numbers of specific glands in normal individuals.

Environments differ. There are individual differences in environments that may be described in terms of differing ability requirements and differing reinforcer characteristics.

Borgen et al. (1968) and Rosen et al. (1972) were able to develop reliable occupational reinforcer patterns that differ for occupational environments.

Dvorak (1935) and the U.S. Department of Labor (1979) developed differential occupational aptitude patterns (ability-requirement patterns) across occupations, described in the *Dictionary of Occupational Titles* (U.S. Department of Labor, 1977).

Individuals inherently seek to achieve and to maintain correspondence with their environments.

Cannon (1932), in his physiological research, demonstrated a homeostatic (maintenance of balance) mechanism in the internal environment that lies within the human body.

Selye (1946), doing research with animals and humans, found that under conditions of extreme environmental demands, the stress response serves as a balancing mechanism.

In a study of the heritability of psychological needs, as measured by the MIQ, Bergmark (1988) demonstrated high levels of heritability for some needs, such as ability utilization, social status, variety, and security, suggesting a genetic basis for reinforcer requirements (preferences).

Anderson (1969) found that significantly higher proportions of individuals unable to achieve satisfaction in their jobs than those who were satisfied left their jobs.

The achievement by an individual of correspondence in his or her environment results in adjustment, that is, satisfaction by an individual and satisfactoriness of the individual.

Betz (1969) predicted satisfaction from the correspondence of psychological needs and reinforcer patterns in a work environment.

Rounds (1981) predicted later satisfaction in occupations chosen in counseling on the basis of correspondence between psychological needs and occupational reinforcer patterns for clients who also meet the ability requirements of the occupation.

Carlson et al. (1969) were able to forecast satisfactoriness of workers from data on the correspondence of abilities and ability requirements.

Validity studies, such as those reported by Ghiselli (1966) and Dvorak (1935), have demonstrated that satisfactoriness may be predicted from the correspondence of abilities and ability requirements.

Because individuals interact with a number of main environments, it is important to identify the salience of environments in terms of both frequency of problems and importance to the individual.

Chartrand (1988), studying a sample of continuing education and graduate students, reported data that support the assertion that environments differ in salience for different individuals.

Psychological needs are developed and shaped by an individual's experiences in a response and reinforcement history.

Research by Rounds et al. (1979) demonstrated that profiles of psychological needs similar to profiles based on measured needs using the MIQ can be forecast from biographical data for a female sample. The study also indicated that there are sex differences in the items that are effective in forecasting for males and females.

Personality style dimensions, as indicators of when and how an individual is likely to act, are useful personality descriptors for the interaction between personality-structure and the environment.

Humphrey (1980) found the adjustment-style dimensions of flexibility, activeness, and reactiveness to be valid constructs and to be relatively independent dimensions. Low-level relationships were found for activeness and reactiveness, and for flexibility and activeness. A stronger relationship was found between reactiveness and flexibility.

Pioneering research on the establishment of thresholds of flexibility (tolerance of discorrespondence) by Cheung (1975) is promising.

Chapter 5

Developmental Antecedents of Concepts in the P-E-C Theory

By examining the etiology of the major sets of personality dimensions, one may more fully appreciate the strength and power of personality-structure and personality-style dimensions. In our description of personality, abilities and values, the reference dimensions for skills and needs, have been defined as the principal sets of dimensions of personality structure. Celerity, pace, rhythm, and endurance, typical ways of responding, have been defined as the principal personality-style dimensions.

Interests have been described as the products of interaction between abilities and values. Adjustment-style dimensions have been defined as flexibility, activeness, reactiveness, and perseverance.

The inherent striving of individuals to achieve and maintain correspondence with environmental conditions is the motivational wellspring for continuous behavioral interaction across several major environments containing several different kinds of stimulus conditions. This continuous behavioral interaction from birth to physical maturity establishes levels and patterns of the major personality dimensions to form a crystallized personality that is observable and reliably measurable for most individuals at about the attainment of physical maturity.

The paragraphs that follow describe our conceptualization of the origin and development of these major personality dimensions.

Origin of Abilities

In the development of abilities, each individual begins with hereditary potential that sets the limits for development. Within this potential, the individual sets out on a developmental road that leads to the establish-ment of a mature set of abilities on which to draw for response capability for meeting the requirements of environments.

In the earliest portion of building a response and reinforcement history, in infancy, the individual is stimulated physiologically and physically. Re-sponsive behavior is elicited by this stimulation. As the individual satisfies these physiological and physical demands of self and the early environ-ment, he or she reaches out and moves on to test, try out, and explore the environment and begins to act on the environment. That is, individual be-havior now is emitted, with stimulation following on response action. The consequences of acting on the environment under specific stimulus condi-tions are experienced as pleasant or unpleasant. The behaviors are posi-tively or negatively reinforced with affective consequences or degrees of satisfaction or dissatisfaction with the results of responding, i.e., the rein-forcement. Over repeated emitted responses, the individual develops and refines many skills out of underlying ability potentials. As opportunities for responding become available, ability potentials are drawn on differentially, in terms of both combinations and levels, in the development of skills. The development of ability dimensions becomes better defined following pro-tracted use of skills in responding. As more skills are developed and re-fined, more combinations are possible and the individual has available a repertoire of response capabilities for meeting a variety of environmental demands.

Early stages of ability development take place in family and social envi-ronments. These are followed by increasingly heavy exposure to educa-tional environments, and then by early work and community environ-ments.

One can also think of the development of abilities in terms of what we can call *content areas* and *process areas*. The content areas include the de-velopment of symbolic abilities, interpersonal abilities, and sensorimo-tor abilities, which are sometimes termed data, people, and things abil-ities, respectively. On the process area side, there is development of afferent abilities for sensation and perception; mediational abilities for cognition, memory, reasoning, and judgment; and efferent or motor action abilities. These three process areas can also be thought of as process areas that deal with input, central processing, and output abilities, respectively.

Given the long, powerful, and varied reinforcement history of response and reinforcement experienced by most mature adults, and the fact that the crystallized set of ability dimensions shows little fluctuation in level and pattern, it is probably not feasible to expect that this set of basic personality-structure dimensions will be changed through counseling or therapy. It is probably much more reasonable to concentrate on improving knowledge of response capabilities, how to use them in environments, how to present them to environments, and how to find or change environments or change the self style to present a better fit (improved correspondence). We feel that these same caveats apply as well to the other personality structure and style dimensions that have been identified.

Origin of Values

As an individual experiences the consequences of responding in certain stimulus conditions throughout a reinforcement history, stimulus conditions found to have positive or negative reinforcement, pleasing or displeasing affect, are remembered by the individual. The individual classifies these experiences in terms of similarity of stimulus conditions. With many experiences with similar conditions, the classification becomes more definitive. Examples of such classes based on similarity are situations where dealing with people was positively reinforced, or where taking responsibility or showing creativity was reinforced with positive affective consequences. Classes of similar situations where negative reinforcement was experienced will also be established. The individual over time develops a set of preferences for responding in situations that belong to positively experienced classes of stimulus conditions. Individuals also learn to avoid situations that have been experienced as aversive. Levels and patterns of preferences across these classes of conditions are established, become stable, and are measurable. They are called psychological needs and are translated into reference dimensions called values. Values are a major set of personality-structure dimensions. The development of needs and values takes place concurrently and in conjunction with the development of skills and abilities.

Origin of Personality Style

Over a long history of responding, individuals learn what is adequate for quickness of response (celerity), level of effort (pace), pattern of effort (rhythm), and duration of response (endurance) with respect to the majority of typical response situations. "Adequate" is the level necessary to avoid interference with expected reinforcement. Over time, the individual develops habitual and typical ways of responding that can be measured on these personality-style dimensions.

Origin of Adjustment Style

Individuals differ on a dimension of flexibility, which is defined as tolerance for discorrespondence. In seeking a person-environment fit, individuals will rarely or never experience perfect correspondence; in other words, some degree of discorrespondence is experienced. Different degrees of satisfaction are experienced with different levels of correspondence with the environment. Over a long period of experience with levels of correspondence, the individual develops a standard for evaluating the amount of correspondence that the individual must require for minimal satisfaction.

This standard sets the threshold for tolerance of discorrespondence. If a situation is discorrespondent enough to exceed the threshold for tolerance, the individual is moved to use adjustment modes in an attempt to redress the discorrespondence. Two major adjustment modes are activeness, acting on the environment to change it to reduce discorrespondence, and reactiveness, acting on self to change presentation of personality to reduce discorrespondence.

Because environments change and individuals develop throughout their response and reinforcement histories, adjustment comes into constant play. With protracted experience, individuals learn about the effectiveness of each of the adjustment modes in bringing about change that results in more correspondence. Individuals differ in their disposition to act on the environment or on self. These dispositions for action to improve correspondence stabilize and can be measured. Individuals will also differ in how long they will pursue adjustment modes before leaving the environment because of discorrespondence—that is, they differ in perseverance.

Origin of Interests

Throughout an individual's reinforcement history, the response-reinforcement interaction occurs in the context of activities. Following exposure of the individual to a variety of such activity settings, the individual begins to develop preferences for some activities over others. Such preferences probably arise out of the individual's capability in carrying out the activity and the reinforcement value of the stimulus conditions that are presented in the activity. Interests can be viewed as preferences for activities that are products of interaction between abilities and values. These preferences for activities become crystallized and stable and can be measured reliably. Interests are different from needs in that interests are preferences for activities as a whole, whereas needs are preferences for stimulus conditions for response.

The measurement of interests at this time is broader in its sampling of activities and other preferences than would typically be experienced by an individual, e.g., a broad range of occupations and a number of hobbies. Preferences for such nondirectly experienced activities probably derive from knowledge gained from reading, from observation of the preferences of role models, peers, and family, and from stereotypes that we all hold about the nature of activities we have not experienced.

Origins of Presenting Problems

The theses that underlie the P-E-C Theory of Counseling are that individuals inherently seek (are motivated) to achieve and maintain correspondence with their environments, and that presenting problems have their roots in person-environment discorrespondence. When an individual perceives discorrespondences that allow less than satisfaction, descriptions and symptoms of displeasure, dissatisfaction, unhappiness, and tension arise, and the individual seeks help through counseling or other means. The individual's description of his or her displeasure or dissatisfaction at the time help is sought is called the presenting problem. The origin of the presenting problem lies in individual perception of lack of P-E fit (discorrespondence) based on both actual correspondence between personality and environment and desired fit between the individual's self-image and the environment.

It is very important to note that there is more than one kind of P-E correspondence. One must assess both objective correspondence or discorrespondence (i.e., measured correspondence based on comparison of objective personality and environment measurements) and subjective correspondence (i.e., self-reported experience of correspondence). The perceptual screen through which an individual views objective (measured) reality may distort the individual's assessment of how well or how poorly personality and environment complement each other and may affect behavior in the environment and spill over to create some difficulties with adequate functioning in other environments.

There seem to be at least three kinds of perceptions of correspondence that an individual might demonstrate:

accurate subjective evaluation (perception) of the objective correspondence derived from knowledge of personality and environment characteristics not influenced by outside pressures or by an unrealistic self-image

inaccurate (distorted) evaluation of objective reality stemming from lack of knowledge of personality and environment characteristics, including inability to comprehend requirement and reinforcement conditions that are present in the environment

inaccurate (distorted) evaluation of the correspondence with the objectively described environment stemming from an unrealistic self-image (developed without enough testing of reality) that is neither consonant with the objectively measured personality nor what can realistically be expected by anyone in an environment typical of the one in question

Some simplistic but often powerful examples of distorted perceptions arising from outside pressures might include strong pressures from peers or family: "Be something more, get ahead, make something more of yourself," or "They don't treat you well in that job," or "Other people's spouses give a lot more support to their partners; maybe you should make a change." An unrealistic self-image that is not in concert with personality potentials and limits might result from untested belief that one can do whatever is desired if one only believes it and puts forth the effort. Such an unwise belief is reminiscent of the "log cabin to the White House" philosophy that existed early in this century and that paid no attention to individuals' potentials and limits and the limits of opportunity.

Chapter 6

The Counseling Process

Before describing the counseling process as we visualize it in P-E-C counseling, it may be useful to provide a general description of counseling, listing some examples of intervention behaviors available to counselors, describing examples of client behaviors counselors can observe that may serve as indicators of progress in achieving intermediate goals in the process, advancing some diagnostic hypotheses a counselor may wish to explore in the early stages of P-E-C counseling, and listing some preconditions that we feel are necessary for effective counseling.

General Description

Counseling may be described as an interaction between a counselor and a client with a problem in which the counselor, using professional tools and knowledge, works to help the client choose courses of action that are the most likely to result in the solution of the problem. **Counseling is a problem-solving process that focuses on appropriate client choice and client action**.

Counselor-client interaction involves action (influencing) and reaction (changing) on the part of both individuals. Counselor and client both have expectations (requirements) of each other and of the process (the interaction). Movement (progress) in the counseling process depends on the effectiveness of each party as the environment for the other. **Counselor-client interaction is a reciprocal process of responding to requirements**.

Client problems may center on failure to adjust to a current environment or on the desire to find a more satisfying environment (e.g., one with more opportunity for self-expression or fuller manifestation of the personality). These general classes of client problems cut across specific classes of environments, such as vocational, marital, school, social, and retirement. For instance, a client may have difficulty in adjusting to a current work environment or may have difficulty selecting an appropriate work environment in which to express self (personality). A client may have difficulty finding an appropriate person to marry, or may have difficulty adjusting in a marriage. **Client problems require either adjusting to a specific problem environment or finding an alternative environment that is more correspondent**.

The counselor helps the client to understand the nature of the problem by identifying the significant information relevant to the problem. The counselor helps the client to decide on a course of action for solving the problem; that is, the counselor helps the client to make appropriate choices and to act on them. "Appropriateness" of client choice in counseling is based on counselor predictions of adjustment. These predictions are derived from the client's estimate of own satisfaction and the counselor's forecast of both the client's and the environment's requirements being satisfied. When both these conditions are met, adjustment is predicted. **Appropriate client choices are those for which the likelihood of adjustment is highest from among the available alternatives**.

Counselor behavior in the counseling interaction may range, for particular clients, from following the lead of the client, through persuading the client, to directing the client. Client behavior could range from following the counselor's direction, through allowing some counselor direction, to using the counselor only as a provider of information. Counselor and client behaviors are influenced by the individuals' styles in interaction situations, that is, by their tendencies to adjust either by seeking to change the other person or seeking to change self. **Counselor and client behaviors stem in part from the interactive style of each person**.

The client comes for counseling with certain expectations of the counselor that may include seeing the counselor as an expert, seeing the counselor as a friend, seeing the counselor as a decision maker, or seeing the counselor as a helper in decision making. The counselor also has expectations for the client that may include a need for intervention by an expert, a willingness to work with some direction by the counselor, and a capability to weigh alternatives and make decisions. In the counseling process, counselor and client may be considered as environments for each other. Each has requirements of the other, and each may strive to meet the other's requirements. **Counselor and client interaction stems in part from the expectations (requirements) each has of the other**.

The first tasks of the counselor include establishing a relationship, determining client expectations, communicating counselor capabilities and expectations, identifying the problem, and assessing the likely effectiveness of counseling. The first objective of the counselor is to learn more about the problem. This includes learning more about the context of the problem, which entails learning more about the client and about the environment in which the problem is centered. This requires counselor professional skill in the assessment of both individuals and environments. It also requires counselor skills in communicating information to a particular client and in fostering acceptance of the information. **Given a working understanding of the problem, the counselor and client will explore alternative approaches to solving the problem**.

As each alternative is considered, additional information may be required for the fullest appreciation of the alternative. The counselor and client can then decide on the best alternative. The client should then be fully aware of the rationale for the particular choice. **The counselor's primary task is to bring the client to the point of making an informed choice that has a good chance of success**.

Making a choice behaviorally includes acting on the intention. The counselor may help the client to plan the action required by the decision. The formal counseling interaction may be concluded at this point. The counselor should, however, provide for some follow-up of the client's progress after counseling. Follow-up data on outcomes give the counselor general feedback, provide a means for assessing the effectiveness of specific techniques and instruments, and should lead to improvement of counselor skills and resources. **Evaluation of the outcomes of counseling is an essential final task of the counselor**.

Examples of Counselor Intervention Behaviors

There are many possible intervention behaviors available to counselors. Some intervention behaviors counselors might use to effect progress in counseling are as follows:

1. Employ active listening.
2. Show empathy, positive regard, and sincerity.
3. Demonstrate understanding.
4. Adopt attentive body language.
5. Restrict amount of counselor talk to facilitate client talk.
6. Use a conversational level that fits the client's ability levels, knowledge, and comfort.
7. Structure nature and length of counseling interviews.
8. Assign client tasks to assure client is the more active participant in problem solving in the counseling process.
9. Ask client to summarize important points and progress at the end of interviews.
10. Assign homework to give client experience in generating relevant information and data for decision making.
11. Provide and describe assessment tools and instruments.
12. Confront client on inaccurate perceptions.
13. Teach client adjustment skills.
14. Provide client with rubrics for assessing personality and environment characteristics.
15. Suggest useful reference materials.
16. Suggest places and individuals where additional information relevant to decision making may be available.

17. Accept the role of an authority figure, with some disclosure of previous experience with particular strategies.

18. Use selective reinforcement to facilitate client movement in problem solving and decision making.

19. Foster increasing client independence as the counseling process moves ahead.

20. Demonstrate satisfaction (positive affect) with significant client achievements.

Client Behaviors as Progress Indicators

A client may have feelings about progress being made in counseling and may or may not report them. These reports are useful but may not be sufficient. In order to manage the counseling process effectively, the counselor needs objective (behavioral) indicators of progress. Following are some client behaviors that may be used as indicators of progress:

1. Client talk increases.

2. Problem relevance of client talk increases.

3. Client acknowledges accuracy of counselor reflection and paraphrasing.

4. Client responds positively to counselor interpretation, an indication of perceiving counselor understanding.

5. Client schedules and appears for subsequent interviews.

6. Client completes assigned tasks and homework.

7. Client describes behavior in main general environments.

8. Client describes feelings about behavior in main general environments.

9. Client completes hierarchy of main general environments based on frequency and intensity of perceived problems.

10. Client decides on the ordering of environments by problem frequency and intensity after comparing client and counselor hierarchies.

11. Client completes extensive biographical information form.

12. Client completes a hierarchy of main general environments based on their importance for ideal adjustment.

13. Client decides on final environment importance hierarchy.

14. Client completes psychometric assessment of abilities and psychological needs.

15. Client is able to paraphrase counselor interpretation of psychometric test results as descriptors of personality.

16. Following discussion of environmental salience based on both problem and importance hierarchies, client makes a decision on the target environment(s) to be addressed in the counseling process.

17. Client finds support for choice of target environment(s) in biographical data on own past behaviors in similar main general environment(s).

18. Client constructs requirement and reinforcer system profiles for the target environment(s) using the same rubrics that were employed in the psychometric sampling of personality characteristics.

19. Client accurately locates discrepancies between personality dimensions (abilities and needs) and the characteristics (requirements and reinforcers) of the target environment.

20. Client demonstrates learning of use of adjustive modes (activeness, reactiveness, or both) by verbal report and by acting them out in environmental homework assignments.

21. Client reports progress in adjustments to specific discorrespondences between self and the target environment.

22. Client shows increasing positive affect (satisfaction) for the current response and reinforcement conditions in the target environment.

23. Client verbal behavior and affective state (satisfaction) indicate decrease in number and intensity of problems client originally perceived as associated with the presenting problem.

24. Client demonstrates learning that the presenting problem did not just arise by itself, but very likely had its roots in person-environment discorrespondence.

25. Client reports continuing use of adjustment modes in some degree, an indication of the likelihood of potential for maintaining continuing adjustment.

26. Client agrees that formal counseling should be discontinued.

27. On follow-up, client indicates little or no recurrence of the original presenting problem.

Diagnostic Hypotheses for Exploration in P-E-C Counseling

In the P-E-C approach to counseling, emphasis is placed on the identification of P-E discorrespondence from which the presenting problems arise. It may be useful in the initial stages of counseling for the counselor to entertain some hypotheses about the possible roots of client problems. Following are some hypotheses the counselor may wish to explore:

1. There is discorrespondence between objective abilities and requirements.

    Abilities are lower than ability requirements.

    Abilities are higher than ability requirements.

2. There is discorrespondence between subjective ability-requirement appraisal and objective ability-requirement measurements.

    Abilities are perceived as higher than measured.

    Abilities are perceived as lower than measured.

    Tasks are perceived as more difficult than they actually are.

    Requirements are perceived as less than they actually are.

3. Correspondence of abilities and requirements but with inadequate performance may reflect recent changes resulting in discorrespondence in general environments other than the target environment.

4.   Correspondence of abilities and requirements but with inadequate performance may be a result of dissatisfaction with need-reinforcer system discorrespondence.

5.   There is discorrespondence between measured psychological needs and objective reinforcers.

Reinforcers are lower than need levels.

Reinforcers are higher than need levels.

Stated need-reinforcer discorrespondence may be a rationalization for abilities being lower than ability requirements.

6.   Preferences measured as psychological needs may be projections of strong self-image factors arrived at vicariously through a somewhat impoverished reinforcement history with limited reality testing. Such preferences may not be substantiated by inferences from biographical data.

7.   Satisfactoriness and satisfaction indicate adequate personality-environment correspondence and counseling presenting problem is seen as a way of coping with outside pressures (from spouse, peers, social group, family, work).

Preconditions for Counseling

The preconditions listed below may seem obvious and trivial, but it is necessary that counselors observe them and commit to them. They also have special importance for the selection and training of counseling students.

The client:

states a problem;

desires professional assistance; and

is able to communicate.

The counselor:

has expertness, knowledge, and skill in establishing and maintaining relationships, in assessment, in counseling techniques, and in teaching;

has commitment to human dignity;

believes in individual differences;

respects the individual's status across economic, social, educational, and occupational strata, and sex and race;

is committed to the privacy of the client and the confidentiality of the client-counselor relationship;

has self-knowledge of own personality (including needs and capabilities); and

provides for the client's physical and psychological comfort.

The Counseling Process

In the description that follows, the counseling process is detailed by the use of brief descriptions of counselor behaviors (counselor interventions, using the term broadly) and by the provision of examples of client behaviors that may be used as indicators of the achievement of intermediate goals in the process. While the description includes the use of many common counselor practices, its main focus is on the use of the Person-Environment-Correspondence Theory. The process is broken down into several phases to highlight counselor-client goals. These "stages" in the process are not intended to be equated with separate interviews or to be achieved always in single interviews. While they highlight areas to be covered in the counseling, they are somewhat artificial in that their occurrence will depend on factors such as the extent and intensity of client problems and the level of client motivation and participation.

Stage 1. Establishing a Working Client-Counselor Relationship

Counselor Behaviors

Greets client in a cordial but professional manner.

Introduces self using full name and title.

Addresses client by full name until preference is known.

Provides a comfortable, open, and private setting for interviews.

Asks client to describe situation that led to working with counselor.

Listens actively.

Shows empathy, positive regard, and sincerity.

Uses reflection of feelings.

Adopts attentive body language.

Elicits client talk by using reflection and paraphrasing.

Restricts own talk to facilitate client talk.

Uses interpretation to demonstrate understanding.

Uses some questions of the "Tell me more" variety.

Explains need for taking notes for use in later discussion.

Asks client to summarize the problem(s) he or she has presented.

Describes need for and length of interviews.

Emphasizes expectation of full client and counselor participation.

Describes the P-E-C counseling approach to problems.

Describes generally the availability of useful assessment tools.

Assigns completion of biographical data form as homework.

Assigns the listing of some problem-related incidents as homework.

Schedules an appointment for the next interview.

Terminates the interview by noting that next time the biographical information and list of problem incidents will serve to help in exploration of the problem that exists.

Indicators of Achievement of Intermediate Goals

Client talk ratio increases.

Problem relevance of client talk increases.

Client acknowledges accuracy of counselor reflection and paraphrasing.

Positive client response to counselor interpretation indicates perception of counselor understanding.

Client's summary of first interview is generally accurate.

Client schedules a second interview.

Client appears for second and subsequent interviews.

Client completes assigned homework tasks.

Stage 2. Exploring the client's problem (nature, intensity, locale)

Counselor Behaviors

Reviews and expands biographical information with client.

Reviews list of problem-related incidents with client.

Continues to show empathy, positive regard, sincerity, and understanding.

Explores client behaviors and client perception of consequences across several major environments.

Seeks client identification of environments in which client perceives most problems.

Asks client to rate environments according to the number and intensity of problems encountered.

Rates environments according to number and intensity of problems.

Discusses with the client the similarities and differences of ratings by the client and by the counselor of the hierarchies for main general environments according to number and intensity of problems experienced.

Uses interpretation, summarization, and perhaps confrontation to facilitate client identification of the target problem environment for which person-environment correspondence should be addressed.

Requests client to rate general environments for importance of satisfactory and satisfying adjustment.

Compares with the client the target environment from a problem standpoint with the ratings of environments most important for adjustment, to assess likely motivation for adjustment in the target environment.

Asks client to provide more information about general adjustment by asking questions such as "Can you tell me more about what you do (at work, at home, at school, in social situations)?" "How do you feel about yourself in this environment so that we can both get a larger picture of how you feel your life is going; that is, how satisfying do you find these different environments?"

Facilitates client decisions that lead to being motivated to work on problems in the target environment.

Asks client to complete an environmental satisfaction questionnaire for the target environment.

Indicators of Achievement of Intermediate Goals

Client continues interviews.

Client completes rating tasks assigned as homework.

Client decides on environmental problem and importance hierarchies.

Client and counselor agree on the target environment.

Stage 3. Assessing Client Personality and Self-Image

Counselor Behaviors

Describes psychological tests used to assess ability and need dimensions and interests.

Facilitates client decision to take the assessment instruments by giving examples of how they will be used to address problems of discorrespondence.

Asks client to rate how he or she would measure up on each of the ability and need dimensions to be assessed, providing the client rubrics on which to make the estimates and a normative basis for making the ratings.

Administers the psychological assessment instruments to the client.

Discusses client ratings on personality dimensions to make inferences about the state of the client's self-image of personality.

Interprets assessment-test results to the client and asks for client appraisal of the accuracy of the test information.

Compares with the client the personality dimension estimates by the client with the measured levels on the personality dimensions to make an assessment of the degree of accuracy of the self-image the client brings to an environmental interaction and to make inferences about the kind of screen (self-image) through which the client is likely to view environmental requirements and environmental reinforcers.

Uses interpretation and confrontation, if necessary, to modify discorrespondent aspects of the client's self-image so that they are in reasonable accord (correspondent) with the objectively measured personality.

Indicators of Achievement of Intermediate Goals

Client completes ratings of personality dimensions as a homework assignment.

Client completes psychometric assessment of abilities and needs.

Client is able to paraphrase and summarize counselor interpretation of psychometric test results as a description of personality.

Client is able to describe self-image in reasonably accurate terms.

Stage 4. Assessing the Target Environment in Personality Terms

Counselor Behaviors

Obtains data on environmental requirements and reinforcers for the target environment from previous research, observation, expert raters, or inference from relevant data in existing taxonomies.

Describes ability requirements and reinforcer system of the target environment to the client in the same terms that abilities and needs in the client's personality were measured and described.

Asks the client to describe ability and need discorrespondences and correspondences when self-image and target environment are compared.

Asks client to think about what actions might be taken by acting on self or on the environment to reduce discorrespondence if it appears that remedial action is feasible and the discorrespondence is not extreme enough to warrant changing to a different environment.

Explains the concept of personality style.

Asks client to complete the personality-style checklist and, as homework, to jot down critical incidents that describe styles.

Scores and discusses personality-style checklist and discusses style of behavior in incidents reported by the client.

Explains concept of adjustment style.

Facilitates client-counselor agreement on adjustment style most likely to be effective for action (activeness, reactiveness, or both).

Discusses examples of ways in which the client might act on self or environment to reduce specific discorrespondences and what the responses of the target environment might be.

Asks client to use agreed-upon adjustment style and to note responses of the target environment that can then be discussed further after a period between interviews has elapsed.

Discusses effects of actions on self or environment and asks for client assessment of any changes in correspondence and in satisfaction with the interaction with the target environment.

In cases where discorrespondence is extreme, suggests client may wish to consider leaving the environment and may wish to identify alternate possible and more correspondent environments.

In cases where there is adequate personality-environment correspondence but client dissatisfaction, explores with client other factors that may be precluding perception of a satisfying interaction, such as family pressure, peer pressure, or dislike of the style of a significant person in the environment.

If other factors are operating when correspondence should be satisfying, asks client to consider changes in personality-style behaviors that may provide remedies.

Asks client to summarize the state of person-environment correspondence that has been discussed, the style behaviors taken or contemplated, and the perceived effects of such behaviors on overall satisfaction.

Indications of Achievement of Intermediate Goals

Client's description of self-environment correspondence is accurate.

Client completes homework on personality-style checklist and supporting incidents.

Client accurately describes own personality-style behaviors.

Client chooses adjustment-style actions to be used.

Client brings in a report on the effects of adjustment-style actions taken in interaction with the target environment.

Client becomes active in the exploration and choice of alternate environments where change is clearly necessary.

Client accurately summarizes state of person-environment correspondence and the adjustment actions that are designed to improve correspondence.

Client reports increased satisfaction following change in personality-style behaviors.

Stage 5. Assessing the Effect of Counseling on the Presenting Problem

Counselor Behaviors

Asks client to describe the presenting problem that led to this series of counseling interviews.

Asks client to describe the current state of his or her problems.

Asks client to compare original presenting problem with current state of problems, describing similarities and differences as fully as possible.

Administers an environmental satisfaction questionnaire for discussion and comparison with the one administered in the problem-exploration stage of the interviews.

Offers the client the opportunity for follow-up interviews if desired to facilitate the maintenance of the degree of correspondence that has been achieved.

Asks client permission to send follow-up questionnaires at a later date.

Indications of Achievement of Intermediate Goals

Client describes original problem that led to counseling.

Client describes current state of problems as minimal or as reduced in number and intensity.

Client completes MSQ-G as requested.

Client's current satisfaction with the target environment measures significantly higher than in the problem-exploration stage of the counseling process.

Client gives permission to send follow-up questionnaires at a later date and signs informed consent form.

In this brief description of a counseling process that may be followed when using the P-E-C approach, we have focused on positive client responses to counselor interventions to indicate responses of the client to progessively more important intermediate goals, and to provide examples of benchmarks of client-counselor achievements as the process develops. Descriptions of the several necessary assessment instruments used in the process are described in Chapter 8.

Chapter 7

The Self-Image in P-E-C Theory

Inasmuch as the self-image is a set of perceptions of self by an individual, accuracy of the self-image when compared with measured personality, its motivational effects, and its susceptibility to change when required by reality factors are essential ingredients in the P-E-C approach to counseling. Our view of self-image is presented in the following paragraphs.

Definition

The self-image is the individual's perception of his or her personality, that is, of his or her psychological needs and values and of abilities for satisfying those needs and values in interactions with the main general environments (e.g., work, social, educational, family) that life presents. It is an individual's subjective appraisal of the major sets of personality variables that he or she possesses in some degree and combination, that is, of psychological needs that reflect reinforcer preferences for responding, and of general and specific abilities that underlie capability to respond to environmental requirements. This subjective appraisal is shaped by knowledge gained from experience in a total reinforcement history, by aspirations and goals, and, quite likely, by the current pressures of daily living, such as those stemming from social situations, family, peers, and economic status. The perception of self is also likely to be affected by such factors as emulation of role models, limited stereotypical information about the nature of requirements and reinforcers in particular environments, some fantasizing, and social desirability of role status in a general environment.

Importance

The self-image has powerful motivational implications. Its set of ap-
praised personality dimensions provides "knowledge" on which to base
convictions and aspirations. It provides a basis for feelings that speak to
such matters as "who I am," "what I want to do," "what I can accomplish," and "what I expect from environments for satisfaction with life."
The self-image provides the context for the individual's more specific
agenda for response in, and expections of, environments. Acting on the
more specific agenda for responding and expectation tests the self-image
against reality factors. This reality testing results in varying degrees of
adjustment of the individual to the environment, that is, varying
amounts of satisfactoriness of response and of satisfaction with reinforcement.

Accuracy

Given that individuals inherently seek to achieve correspondence with
their environments and that adjustment is a function of correspondence
between personality characteristics and environment characteristics, it
becomes imperative that individuals know themselves accurately and
project self-images that accurately reflect the personality characteristics
that they will test in environmental reality. This is necessary both to
identify appropriate environments and to function in them in a satisfactory and satisfying, adjusted, fashion. There are individual differences
in the accuracy of individuals' self-images. *Accuracy* here refers to reasonable correspondence of the self-image to the objective (measured)
personality, or perception of self in terms concordant with the individual's sets of personality dimensions. The criterion against which accuracy is assessed is the objectively measured personality. Reasonable correspondence of self-image to personality could be thought of as
correspondence within the range of the probable error of measurement
on the personality dimensions. Establishing the accuracy of client self-

image and facilitating client achievement of accuracy are necessary intermediate goals in the P-E-C counseling process.

The importance of self-image accuracy lies in the role of the self-image in establishing the perceptual screen through which the individual views correspondence between the personality and the environment. Inaccuracy of self-image generates inaccurate perception of the correspondence between actual self (personality) and reality (environment) and leads to a distorted view of objectively measured correspondence or discorrespondence. In most counseling cases, some shaping of the self-image for improved accuracy is important; in some cases, drastic restructuring or even development of the self-image is necessary. Reshaping and restructuring require assessment of the existing self-image and personality, client interpretation of the comparisons, and reinforcing accurate self-perceptions in order to shape perceptions in the direction of increased correspondence with the objective facts. Figure 7.1 depicts the self-image in the Person-Environment-Correspondence model.

Assessment

Although the description of the self-image poses more difficulties for the counselor and client than objective personality description, where direct measurement of abilities and needs based on performance of tasks (test items) is possible, there are a number of ways in which the problem can be approached.The client may, for example, be asked to estimate levels and patterns of psychological needs and abilities. Prior to actual measurement of personality, the client estimates levels of psychological needs that would be satisfied in an environment that is ideal in terms of compatibility with self. Using a rubric of psychological needs like the one presented in the MIQ, and following an alternation-ranking procedure, the client produces a hierarchy of importance of needs for self. In order to estimate the differences in levels of importance of the psychological needs more accurately, the client then assigns each of them to a level on the MIQ profile. The resulting estimated needs profile can also *(note, top)* ✱ if satisfactoriness exists and satisfaction is experienced, there is no need for adjustment

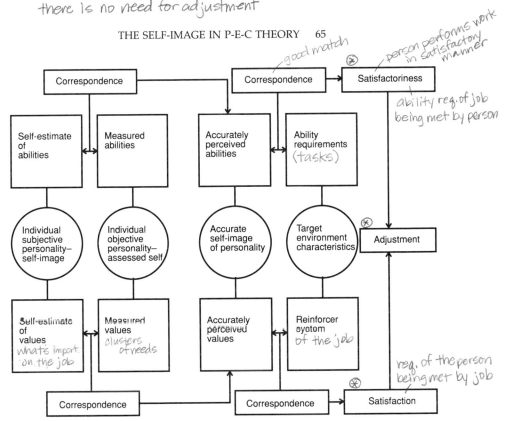

(annotations on figure) good match ✱ / person performs work in satisfactory manner / ability req. of job being met by person / req. of the person being met by job

Figure 7.1. The Self-image in the Person-Environment-Correspondence model

be viewed in terms of clusters of underlying needs—that is, in terms of values.

The client can also estimate levels of ability possessed on the basis of comparing self with a general-population norm group in terms of estimated ability-level placements in percentiles or in quartiles, from highest to lowest 25% of the population. A rubric like the one presented in the GATB can be used to ensure meaningful breadth of principal ability dimensions. These estimation procedures should be completed prior to the measurement of abilities. The need and ability estimates provide descriptive data about the expectations and capabilities of the client in terms of the structure of self as perceived by the client. The estimation procedure also proves useful in preparing the client for the administration of psychological tests, inasmuch as counselor and client will have discussed and clarified the content of the rubrics used in the estimation. Discussion of client experiences supporting client estimations will yield additional data for understanding the client and provide bases for examining correspondence of self as perceived against personality as measured, and for shaping self-image in the direction of maximal correspondence with personality.

Using another approach to the assessment of self-image, counselor and client may examine and discuss biographical history items, such as an occupation or occupational cluster in which the client had substantial tenure, or educational attainments and preferences for school subjects. The tenure in an occupation would imply that the client was at least minimally satisfactory and satisfied (i.e., adjusted). If occupational history data are used, the counselor could locate useful descriptions of minimum occupational ability requirement levels and reinforcer systems in a taxonomy of work such as MOCS III. It should be possible to make rather accurate inferences about ability and need levels and to explore whether or not they are perceived by the client as elements in the current self-image.

The client may wish to take a satisfaction questionnaire, such as the MSQ, focusing on current job or last job, so that inferences can be made about the client's currently perceived need structure. Discussion should lead to additional inferences about the client's current perception of his or her abilities.

In yet another approach, the client may be asked to write down five or six statements that describe "what I like to do and can do best." For instance, a client might write: "I find I can talk convincingly to people to present my own ideas"; or "I am the kind who likes to work with numbers—words are something else"; or "I like to draw things, make designs, and create new shapes." Statements such as these may be discussed to flesh out their full meanings and perhaps generate additional self-statements. The client's sketch of likes and capabilities can then be analyzed by the client and the counselor to identify estimated underlying need and ability patterns, perceived as the structure of the self-image.

Another approach might be to ask the client to consider the worker function lists for Data, People, Things that are presented in the *Dictionary of Occupational Titles*, asking, "Which ones fit me best?" and "Which functions do I like the most?" The client may check the work functions that are chosen or do an alternation ranking for each of the three lists of worker functions. Because the lists present hierarchies of function complexity, they may well provide a good basis for inference of client perceptions of self-ability levels. The worker functions chosen or ranked high will also provide clues to psychological needs perceived to be important parts of the self-image. The client-counselor discussion following choices or ranking will probably be most fruitful if it explores the data-people-things functions against the background of rubrics such as those used in the GATB and the MIQ.

Other sources of useful self-image data include client disclosure in the normal course of interviews, client descriptions by teachers, family, and peers, and institutional records of behavior.

We are not suggesting that the counselor use all of the assessment approaches suggested above with all clients. Some may be more appropriate for a given client than others. The first suggestion—client estimation of abilities and needs— should probably be used with most clients. It is a relatively direct approach to self-image status on personality dimensions and provides for a straightforward comparison with measurement data.

Change

Shaping or restructuring the self-image to increase accuracy—that is, reasonable approximation of the objectively measured personality—is one of the most difficult tasks in counseling. It is likely that the client will hold on tenaciously to the self-image he or she has developed over the years. There are a number of approaches the counselor might take to facilitate client change in perceptions of self with regard to needs and abilities.

At the outset, the counselor should discuss frankly with the client the need for accuracy and the problems likely to arise from inaccuracy, using examples of possible consequences. For example, a client's inaccurate perception of high levels of ability for verbal and numerical tasks coupled with significantly lower levels of these abilities demonstrated when they are measured in the reality of the objective testing situation could well result in that client's perceiving high environmental requirements on these abilities as not being a problem. This could lead to the client's selecting an inappropriate environment, and then attributing lack of successful performance to other nonexistent factors, such as inappropriate supervision or poor working conditions. The odds are good that most clients can think of some instances in which their abilities did not measure up to particular tasks and in which they rationalized their failure in some other way.

The client also has to understand that there are individual differences in ability levels and need levels, and that there is no reason to feel inadequate or depressed over some lower levels of ability. Each individual is unique, with different levels and patterns of abilities and needs, higher on some and lower on others. The key to adjustment is having a reasonably accurate picture of self and identifying the appropriate environments for using self and experiencing adjustment.

Using data from assessment of self-image by estimation, the client can be assigned the homework task of producing self-ability and self-need profiles in the GATB and MIQ frameworks. Similarly, the client may be assigned, as homework, the task of constructing ability and need profiles using data from measured GATB and MIQ dimensions. Self-image profiles should be completed before psychometric measurements are taken. In interviews, the client should be encouraged to take the lead in comparing self-image and measured personality profiles to identify discorrespondences between self-image and personality. The counselor should actively reinforce correct client judgments and selectively withhold reinforcement of inaccurate conclusions. Where the client does not identify discorrespondences that exist, the counselor may have to clarify further what the test results mean and perhaps use confrontational tech-

niques. Where the client seems to be accepting the fact that self-estima-
tions were significantly too high or too low, the counselor will wish to
reflect, paraphrase, and positively reinforce these behaviors as movements toward change for increased accuracy of the self-image.

Where client change is difficult to facilitate in the interview, the counselor may wish to design outside tasks and situations for client reality
testing between interviews that can then be discussed in terms of the
satisfactoriness and satisfaction the client experienced and in the context
of the personality data.

When counselor appraisal indicates the likelihood of shaping or restructuring having taken place, the counselor may wish to have the client complete another set of self-image profiles without the benefit of the
objective assessment data. This assignment may be repeated later in the
process as a reliability check.

In cases where a client significantly underestimates his or her abilities
or demonstrates an underdeveloped need profile, the counselor will
wish to assist the client in finding reality experiences that will allow
some sampling of performance in reality to build confidence in self and
to broaden the experiencing of stimulus situations in which the client
may respond. The counselor can also build client confidence in interviews by concentrating on client achievements in the present situation
and achievements reflected in the available biographical information. In
some extreme cases, client and counselor may need to discuss other
therapeutic approaches or programs, such as assertiveness training.

Figures 7.2 and 7.3 illustrate an approach that the client and counselor
might take when assessing the accuracy of the self-image. The client's
estimations of the levels of abilities and of psychological values he or she
possesses are compared with the measured levels of those same abilities
and values, using instruments such as the GATB and the MIQ. In the
terms of P-E-C Theory, estimated self-image structure is compared with
measured personality structure. Differences arising from the comparison will highlight client overestimates and underestimates, and will provide focus for client-counselor efforts to restructure the self-image for
improved correspondence with the actual personality.

	25%	50%	25%
	Low	Average	High
	0	1	2

Abilities

	Perceptual (P)			Cognitive (C)			Motor (M)		
Abilities	S	P	Q	G	V	N	K	F	M
S-I Estimate	2	1	0	2	2	1	1	2	1
Py Measure	2	1	1	1	2	2	2	2	2
Difference	0	0	−1	+1	0	−1	−1	0	−1

	Perceptual (P)	Cognitive (C)	Motor (M)
Ability Class	P	C	M
Average S-I	1.0	1.7	1.3
Average Py	1.3	1.7	2.0
Difference	−0.3	0	−0.7

Changes indicated to increase S-I/Py correspondence

Decrease S-I level:	Increase S-I level:
_____	_____
_____	_____
_____	_____
_____	_____

Key:
S-I—self-image   Py—personality
S—spatial ability   G—general ability   K—motor coordination
P—form perception   V—verbal ability   F—finger dexterity
Q—clerical perception   N—numerical ability   M—manual dexterity

Note: For ability classes, P is average of S, P, Q; C is average of G, V, N; and M is average of K, F, M.

Figure 7.2. Self-image/Personality Correspondence Indicator

When using the format in Figure 7.3, which deals with values, the counselor would average the scores of the needs related to each value, locate the average scores on the importance scale shown at the top of the figure, convert each value-importance score to the 2-1-0 score, and enter the 2 or 1 or 0 score under the appropriate value designation. This pro-

	−0.5	0.0	0.5	1.0	1.5	2.0	2.5

Not Important	Important	Very Important
0	1	2

Values

Values	Internal (Int)			Social (Soc)	Environmental (Env)	
	ACH	AUT	STA	ALT	COM	SAF
S-I Estimate	___	___	___	___	___	___
Py Measure	___	___	___	___	___	___
Difference	___	___	___	___	___	___

Value Class	Int	Soc	Env
Average S-I	___	___	___
Average Py	___	___	___
Difference	___	___	___

Changes indicated to increase S-I/Py correspondence

Decrease S-I level: Increase S-I level:

_____   _____

_____   _____

_____   _____

Key:
S-I—self-image   Py—personality
ACH—achievement   ALT—altruism
AUT—autonomy   COM—comfort
STA—status   SAF—safety

Values	Needs							
ACH:	AU	___	Ach	___	Ave	___		
AUT:	Cre	___	Res	___	Aut	___	Ave	___
STA:	Adv	___	Rec	___	Au	___	SSt	___	Ave	___
ALT:	CO-G	___	SSe	___	MV	___	Ave	___
COM:	Act	___	Ind	___	Var	___	Com	___	Sec	___
	OpC	___	Ave	___				
SAF:	NP	___	LHR	___	LT	___	Ave	___

Figure 7.3. Self-image/Personality Correspondence Indicator

cedure for obtaining and converting value scores applies to both the estimated (S-I) scores and the measured (Py) scores.

The Role of Measured Interests in P-E-C Counseling

It is important that the self-image also reflect an accurate knowledge of measured interests. This is important to maximizing the adjustment that follows on the achievement and maintenance of P-E correspondence, and in obviating interference with adequate P-E correspondence. We have defined interests as preferences for activities, and have differentiated interests from psychological needs and values. They have not been designated as a basic and principal set of dimensions of personality, as have abilities and values. They are seen here as a very important second-order set of dimensions that support and enhance the prediction of adjustment from ability-requirement and need-reinforcer correspondence.

We have described interests as the product of interaction between abilities and needs. We have also made the point that, given the broad range of activities sampled in interest measurement, and the likelihood of some interest preferences being expressed by individuals who have not experienced an activity, a number of "like" or "dislike" responses may be based only on an individual's visualizing the activity from information gained from secondary sources. These factors do not negate the value of interest testing, but they do cast doubt on the feasibility of clear and direct inference of abilities (or needs) from interest inventory scores alone.

Interest inventories provide clients with accurate information on the similarity of their interests in activities to those of members of specific occupational groups and peers in broader activity groups. While these similarities do not deal directly with ability to perform task requirements or with reinforcement following response to task requirements, they do provide for commonality in a range of other-than-task-related preferences by peers and a real sense of fitting in with groups important to the client.

In career counseling, work-adjustment counseling, and personnel selection, a matching of interests with those of the occupational group for which there is basic P-E correspondence should serve to strengthen and enhance the forecast of client satisfaction. Work also spills over into nonwork social activities, and consonance of the individual in terms of interest similarity should facilitate relationship building, which in turn redounds back to the work situation and may well open up increased opportunity for realization of the work personality.

In marriage counseling, each partner should have knowledge not only of his or her own measured interests, but also the interests of the partner. Similarity of partner interests would not appear to be sufficient by itself for the prediction of adjustment, but may enhance an otherwise correspondent P-E relationship. It seems most important that each partner know the other's pattern and strengths of interests and act to facilitate their realization and to reinforce activities consonant with them.

The client's set of measured interests is seen as an important moderator variable in the predicting of satisfaction from the basic P-E correspondence achieved in the P-E-C counseling process.

Well-standardized instruments for the assessment of interests are available to the client and counselor. Among the most widely used and fully researched inventories are the Strong Interest Inventory (SII; Hansen and Campbell, 1985), the Vocational Preference Inventory (VPI; Holland, 1973), and the Kuder Occupational Interest Survey (KOIS; Kuder, 1977).

Chapter 8
Assessment in Counseling

Assessment is essential to P-E-C counseling as well as to counseling in general. The purpose of assessment is to obtain data to describe individuals and environments as accurately as possible. There are different uses to which assessment data may be put. The data may be used to enhance client self-understanding through counselor interpretation during the counseling process. In this case, communication of these data should minimize the use of technical terms.

Assessment data are also essential for counselor understanding of client problems, for testing diagnostic hypotheses, and for choosing interventions that may resolve the client's problem(s). The counselor will make direct use of data in their more technical forms without needing to communicate methodological or measurement technicalities to the client, unless the client's level of sophistication warrants such communication. Assessment data are also essential to research that counselors should do to evaluate the effectiveness of the counseling process.

There are three main ways of approaching the assessment of an individual or an environment: direct observation, estimation, and inferential methods. Direct observation approaches include direct measurement using valid and reliable psychometric instruments, structured observation using rating and checklist methods, and unstructured observation using case notes to record data. Estimation approaches include judgment methods that rely on raters' knowledge and experience to estimate client and environment standing on specified variables. Inferential approaches entail making deductions from such relevant information as group membership and biographical information, including records of past performance, previous occupations, and educational experiences.

An approach that relies on client self-report provides another source of assessment data. Ordinarily, however, an assessment approach is used to generate data independent of client statements, to provide a basis for evaluating such statements.

Assessment in counseling should, wherever possible, utilize the assessment approach(es) that will yield the most objective data in terms of consistency of interpretation. In this respect, direct observation methods are most preferred. Whereas estimation, inference, and self-report approaches may yield useful data, quality of data decreases as we move down the hierarchy of assessment approaches. Starting at the lowest level of quality of assessment, for example, in the case of interests, we might speak of gradations of quality from stated interests, to manifested (observed) interests, to measured interests, to validated interests (where measured and observed interests correspond). These same levels of quality of assessment may be applied to the assessment of other personality variables such as needs, abilities, and other personality traits.

Whichever assessment methods are adopted, their usefulness depends upon their validity and reliability. Assurance that the method measures what it was designed to measure must be buttressed by counselor information about how well the data derived are related to other relevant measures. Any assessment approach requires more than face validity—that is, it is not enough simply that the approach looks like it is appropriate. Other validity indicators include evidence that the approach can differentiate appropriately between groups (e.g., between an occupational group and a general population group), evidence of the ability to predict outcomes (e.g., to predict academic performance), evidence that the data derived are highly related to data generated for the same purpose using other validated approaches (e.g., raters' estimates of general ability and G on the GATB), and evidence that the content of the instrument samples well the content domain to be represented (e.g., an achievement measure of mathematics should have similar content to what has been learned in the classroom).

There should be evidence of the reliability of the assessment tools that are used. This reliability may come in the form of high correlation between data derived from repeat short-term administration of the same instrument on the same individual or group, high correlation between equivalent forms of the same measure, and high correlation between subsections of the instrument (i.e., internal consistency).

Several caveats for the use of assessment instruments and the data they generate are discussed below.

1. Tests do not measure all of the behavior within a domain. Tests assess a sample of behaviors in a domain, with the sampling designed to tap behaviors across the breadth and depth of the domain. Structured tests accomplish those objectives better than unstructured assessment techniques such as the interview.

2. Assessment data do not provide definitive diagnoses or categorizations; they do provide normative comparisons and other bases for drawing inferences that, taken along with other data, may generate conclusions or hypotheses about an individual.

3. Assessment instruments are not error free. In the interpretation of a score, the counselor must observe the error bands that have been determined for the instrument (e.g., probable error, standard error of measurement). Scores falling within the same error band have to be treated as interchangeable. Error bands must be taken into account in making inferences about the client's present or future status.

4. It is likely that some discrepancies or contradictions between assessment data derived from different instruments or different sources may arise. Exploration of them can enhance understanding of the client and the client's problem.

5. The use of assessment instruments should be carefully prescribed for relevance to the problem(s) at hand. Instruments should not be chosen simply because of their popularity, typical use, or requested use by clients or referring agencies.

6. Proper use of assessment instruments requires training in assessment methodology. Many assessment techniques require the highest level of training for competent use and interpretation.

7. The best assessment instruments require administration according to carefully prescribed standardized procedures. Sending assessment in-

struments home for clients to complete must be avoided. Deviation from prescribed procedures weakens the usefulness of the assessment data.

8. Assessment data given to clients should be in interpreted form. Providing uninterpreted copies of technical data, including profiles, to clients for use in the future may be a disservice if clients lack professional training.

9. Assessment instruments should be administered to clients only when they have been informed of the purpose(s) to be served and they agree to the procedure.

10. Confidentiality of assessment results should be strictly observed.

11. Computerized interpretation of assessment results should be used only when the counselor is certain that there is no danger of overgeneralization from it.

12. Oral and written interpretations of assessment data should be given only to the client.

13. Test instruments and test results require technical interpretation and should not be given to clients. If test results are given to clients for their future use (for good reasons), they should be interpreted for the clients in nontechnical language.

14. The counselor should not use assessment techniques with a client without first preparing the client for their use. Such assessments should not be imposed on the client. Tests should be used only with the client's full agreement, following an explanation of what is to be assessed, and how the assessment is to be accomplished.

15. Tests should be used and interpreted only for the purposes for which they were validated (e.g., interest measures are not designed to be measures of ability).

16. Test interpretation to a client requires a comparison standard. Test scores can be interpreted using a norm or reference group for comparison, or they may be interpreted idiographically, using other scores of the individual as the reference base.

17. If client assessment requires rating procedures, a rubric should be provided that structures, samples, or organizes the domain to be rated.

Instrumentation for the P-E-C Theory

There are several instruments described in the counseling literature that may be used to generate subsets of data necessary for application of the P-E-C model. The descriptions that follow concentrate on those instruments typically used when applying the Theory of Work Adjustment (TWA). There are several reasons for taking this approach. First, there is a base of several years' experience demonstrating the efficacy of this set of instruments. Many of the instruments were developed specifically to assess areas in parallel and comparable terms to facilitate assessment of correspondence, for example, for needs, reinforcers, and satisfaction. Second, the TWA concepts provide, in large part, the central concepts for the Person-Environment-Correspondence Theory of Counseling. The instruments measure dimensions in each of the areas directly and do not require inference from data generated by instruments designed for a different primary use. Finally, it has been possible to adapt the work-adjustment instruments by making minor changes in some items so that they may be applied to several main environments other than work.

Biographical Information Form (BIF)

The BIF is designed to elicit client descriptions of past and present behaviors in a response and reinforcement history that encompasses family, educational, social, and work environments. It has a number of uses in counseling. It generates a broad background of knowledge of the client that provides context for counseling. Client completion of the form is a motivational intervention to stimulate client participation at an early stage of the counseling process.

The BIF provides the client with the opportunity for self-examination of personal history, integration of self-history experiences, and reflection on experiences of behavior over a life span. It provides information on past behaviors that may be used later as a comparison data base for information obtained by psychometric assessment.

Table 8.1. Psychological needs, measured (MIQ) vs. estimated (BIF)

Need Scale	Need scores	
	Measured	Estimated
ACHIEVEMENT	1.4	1.81
1. Ability Utilization	1.4	1.38
2. Achievement	1.3	2.25
COMFORT	−0.1	0.52
3. Activity	−0.7	0.50
4. Independence	−0.7	−1.00
5. Variety	−0.3	0.65
6. Compensation	0.7	0.45
7. Security	−0.5	1.27
8. Working Conditions	0.7	1.25
STATUS	0.2	0.69
9. Advancement	1.3	1.21
10. Recognition	0.7	1.34
11. Authority	−0.5	−0.04
12. Social Status	−0.7	0.26
ALTRUISM	1.2	0.94
13. Co-Workers	0.1	0.86
14. Social Service	1.0	0.59
15. Moral Values	2.5	1.38
SAFETY	0.8	0.43
16. Company Policies	1.5	0.51
17. Supervision—Human Relations	0.5	0.60
18. Supervision—Technical	0.5	0.17
AUTONOMY	0.8	0.74
19. Creativity	1.1	0.66
20. Responsibility	0.5	0.83

Finally, the BIF provides item responses that may be weighted to forecast psychological need and ability profiles for comparison with measured needs and abilities. Tables 8.1 and 8.2 show profiles of an individual's psychological needs and abilities, respectively, as measured and as forecast from the individual's responses on the BIF.

Table 8.2. Abilities, measured (GATB) vs. estimated (BIF)

		Ability score	
Ability Dimension		Measured (GATB)	Estimated (BIF)
G	General Ability	132	132.9
V	Verbal Ability	111	132.9
N	Numerical Ability	129	138.7
S	Spatial Ability	120	115.8
P	Form Perception	98	118.6
Q	Clerical Perception	113	137.2
K	Motor Coordination	111	127.9
F	Finger Dexterity	100	95.5
M	Motor Dexterity	100	99.3

The Minnesota Importance Questionnaire and the General Aptitude Test Battery were used to measure needs and abilities, respectively, for the same individual. The BIF is included in the Appendix.

Minnesota Importance Questionnaire (MIQ, MIQ-G)

The MIQ measures the relative importance for an individual of each of twenty psychological needs (Gay et al., 1971; Rounds et al., 1981). Psychological needs are defined as expressed preferences for responding under specific stimulus conditions in a work environment (MIQ) or in a major general environment (MIQ-G). The questionnaire, in a paired comparison form or an equivalent ranked form, is administered to a client in a formal testing setting. MIQ profiles present scores on each of the twenty needs and on each of six value clusters that underlie the twenty needs. Value scores are useful both for more parsimonious description of the client and for classification purposes when needs/values are used as a classificatory dimension in a taxonomy (e.g., of work).

Administration of the MIQ requires approximately thirty to forty minutes. It has average reliability in the low .80s. Its validity has been shown by its successful use in the prediction of satisfaction, by group-difference data, by factor-analytic studies, and by correlational studies with other instruments.

Table 8.3 presents the needs and need statements for the MIQ, and the corresponding statements in the MSQ and the MJDQ. The MIQ-G is an adaptation of the MIQ for use in general environments. The MIQ-G is reproduced in the Appendix. Table 8.4 shows the statement changes that have been made, as well as the changes for the MSQ-G and the MEDQ.

Minnesota Job Description Questionnaire (MJDQ)
Minnesota Environment Description Questionnaire (MEDQ)

The MJDQ presents a rubric for rating the presence or absence and degree of twenty reinforcers in a work environment. It elicits expert ratings of reinforcer characteristics from immediate supervisors or incumbents. These expert ratings are used to generate occupational reinforcer patterns (ORPs), which differentiate occupations in terms of their reinforcer systems (Borgen et al., 1968). Completion of the MJDQ takes about ten to fifteen minutes. ORPs have been demonstrated to be reliable and valid. The MJDQ has been adapted as the Minnesota Environment Description Questionnaire (MEDQ) for use in nonwork-related situations (see Table 8.4). The MEDQ is reproduced in the Appendix.

Minnesota Satisfaction Questionnaire (MSQ, MSQ-G)

The MSQ measures client satisfaction with need reinforcement in the work environment, using ratings on a five-point scale for twenty reinforcers. It requires about twenty minutes to complete. It has average reliabilities in the high .80s (Weiss et al., 1967), and its validity has been demonstrated in numerous studies. The MSQ has been adapted for use in measuring satisfaction with the reinforcers in a general (nonwork) environment as the MSQ-G (see Table 8.4). A short form of the MSQ-G is presented in the Appendix.

Table 8.3. Scale titles and sample items from the Minnesota Satisfaction Questionnaire, the Minnesota Importance Questionnaire, and the Minnesota Job Description Questionnaire

Scale		MSQ (How satisfied am I with . . .)	MIQ (Which is more important?)	MJDQ (Workers on this job . . .)
1.	Ability Utilization	The chance to make use of my best abilities	I could do something that makes use of my abilities	Make use of their individual abilities
2.	Achievement	The feeling of accomplishment I get from the job	The job would give me a feeling of accomplishment	Get a feeling of accomplishment
3.	Activity	Being able to stay busy	I could be busy all the time	Are busy all the time
4.	Advancement	The chances of advancement in this job	The job would provide an opportunity for advancement	Have opportunities for advancement
5.	Authority	The chance to tell people what to do	I could tell people what to do	Tell other workers what to do
6.	Company Policies and Practices	Company policies and the way they are administered	The company would administer its policies fairly	Have a company that administers its policies fairly
7.	Compensation	How my pay compares with that of other workers	My pay would compare well with that of other workers	Are paid well in comparison with other workers
8.	Co-Workers	The friendliness of my co-workers	My co-workers would be easy to make friends with	Have co-workers who are easy to make friends with
9.	Creativity	The chance to try out some of my own ideas	I could try out my own ideas	Try out their own ideas
10.	Independence	The chance to be alone on the job	I could work alone on the job	Do their work alone
11.	Moral Values	Being able to do the job without feeling it is morally wrong	I could do the work without feeling it is morally wrong	Do work without feeling that it is morally wrong
12.	Recognition	The recognition I get for the work I do	I could get recognition for the work I do	Receive recognition for the work they do
13.	Responsibility	The chance to make decisions on my own	I could make decisions on my own	Make decisions on their own
14.	Security	The way my job provides for steady employment	The job would provide for steady employment	Have steady employment
15.	Social Service	The chance to do things for other people	I could do things for other people	Have work where they do things for other people
16.	Social Status	The chance to be "somebody" in the community	I could be "somebody" in the community	Have a position of "somebody" in the community
17.	Supervision—Human Relations	The way my boss backs up his/her employees (with top management)	My boss would back up the workers (with top management)	Have bosses who back up their workers (with top management)
18.	Supervision—Technical	The way my boss trains his/her employees	My boss would train the workers well	Have bosses who train the workers well
19.	Variety	The chance to do something different every day	I could do something different every day	Have something different to do every day
20.	Working Conditions	The working conditions	The job would have good working conditions	Have good working conditions

Table 8.4. Scale titles and sample items from the Minnesota Satisfaction Questionnaire-G and the Minnesota Importance Questionnaire-G, and the Minnesota Environment Description Questionnaire

Scale	MSQ-G (How satisfied am I with . . .)	MIQ-G (Which is more important?)	MEDQ (People in this environment . . .)
1. Ability Utilization	The chance to make use of my best abilities	I could do something that makes use of my abilities	Make use of their individual abilities
2. Achievement	The feeling of accomplishment I get	I could get a feeling of accomplishment	Get a feeling of accomplishment
3. Activity	Being able to stay busy	I could be busy all the time	Are busy all the time
4. Advancement	The chances of self-advancement	I could have opportunity for self-advancement	Have opportunities for self-advancement
5. Authority	The chance to tell people what to do	I could tell people what to do	Tell other people what to do
6. Co-Group Members	The friendliness of people in my group	People in my group would be easy to make friends with	Are easy to make friends with
7. Compensation	How my rewards compare with those of others	My rewards would compare well with those of others	Are rewarded well in comparison with others
8. Creativity	The chance to try out some of my own ideas	I could try out my own ideas	Try out their own ideas
9. Independence	The chance to be alone	I could be alone	Do things alone
10. Leadership—Human Relations	The way my group leader backs me up	My group leader would back me up	Have group leaders who back them up
11. Leadership—Technical	The way expectations are communicated by the group leader	My group leader would communicate expectations well	Have group leaders who communicate expectations well
12. Moral Values	Being able to do things without feeling they are morally wrong	I could do things without feeling they are morally wrong	Do things without feeling that they are morally wrong
13. Norms and Practices	The way norms and practices are observed	The norms and practices are observed consistently	Have norms and practices that are observed consistently
14. Operating Conditions	The operating conditions	I could have good operating conditions	Have good operating conditions
15. Recognition	The recognition I get for the things I do	I could get recognition for the things I do	Receive recognition for the things they do
16. Responsibility	The chance to make decisions on my own	I could make decisions on my own	Make decisions on their own
17. Security	The way the group provides for my continuing participation	The group would provide for my continuing participation	Have assurance of continuing participation
18. Social Service	The chance to do things for other people	I could do things for other people	Do things for other people
19. Social Status	The chance to be "somebody" in the group	I could be "somebody" in the group	Have a position of "somebody" in the group
20. Variety	The chance to do something different every day	I could do something different every day	Have something different to do every day

Minnesota Satisfactoriness Scales (MSS, MSS-G)

The MSS is an instrument for obtaining ratings of client satisfactoriness in a work environment from supervisors and co-workers. The MSS yields scores for Performance and Conformance as they relate to work environment requirements. It requires approximately ten minutes to administer. Its average reliabilities are in the high .80s. Data from various validity studies are included in the manual (Gibson et al., 1970). The MSS has been adapted for use with general, nonwork environments; the MSS-G is shown in the Appendix.

General Aptitude Test Battery (GATB)

The GATB, developed by Dvorak and the U.S. Employment Service, is a group of twelve tests that measure nine major abilities. These abilities can be grouped into three areas: perceptual (S, P, Q), cognitive (G, V, N), and motor (K, F, M). The GATB was designed to measure individual abilities as they would relate to work environments. Obviously, these abilities have relevance for major environments other than work. GATB scores have also provided the basis for the development of occupational aptitude (ability) patterns by the U.S. Department of Labor. Administration of the GATB requires approximately two and one-fourth hours. An abundance of data on the reliability and validity of the GATB may be found in its manual (U.S. Department of Labor, 1970).

Minnesota Occupational Classification System III (MOCS III)

MOCS III is a taxonomy of work containing descriptive information on occupational reinforcer patterns and occupational ability patterns for use in counseling when work is the target environment. It also provides a basis for inferring the characteristics of retirement environments. It provides a useful framework for classifying other general environments according to their reinforcer systems and ability requirements. A sample taxon from the MOCS III is shown in the Appendix.

Minnesota Ability Rating Scale (MARS)

MARS is an experimental scale that presents a format useful in client estimation of abilities. It utilizes the GATB ability dimensions. As a tool for
client self-estimation of abilities, it provides some insight into the client's
self-image and can be used to assess accuracy of client self-image when
compared with objectively measured abilities. A copy of MARS is included in the Appendix.

Minnesota Ability Requirement Rating Scale (MARRS)

The MARRS is an experimental form for estimating the ability requirements of an environment, using a rubric of the GATB dimensions. The
estimation of requirements by knowledgeable observers provides a basis
for comparing the measured abilities of clients with the environmental
ability requirements. A copy of MARRS is shown in the Appendix.

Minnesota Adjustment Style Checklist (MASC)

The MASC is an experimental form listing phrases and adjectives a
counselor may use to describe the adjustment style of a client. It may be
scored to provide an indicator of adjustment styles (i.e., activeness, reactiveness, and flexibility). A copy of the MASC is shown in the Appendix.

Minnesota Need Estimation Scale (MNES)

The MNES is an experimental form for obtaining clients' rankings of the
importance of reinforcers in an environment to the satisfaction of their
perceived needs. It is reproduced in the Appendix.

Chapter 9
Applying the P-E-C Theory of Counseling

There are several problem areas to which the P-E-C model of counseling can be applied. These include the following:

vocational counseling for career choice

job-adjustment counseling

counseling for job change

vocational rehabilitation counseling

unemployment counseling

marriage counseling

family counseling

stress counseling

addiction counseling

counseling for self-esteem

The theory also has useful applications for psychological retirement counseling, changes in working conditions, job relocation decisions in industry, and planning educational curricula.

Basic Procedures Across Areas

Across the several different problem areas, effective application of the theory requires attention to a common set of basic procedures:

establishment of an accepting and communicative client-counselor relationship

client assessment of self-image

assessment of personality

achievement of a valid self-image

assessment of target environments in personality terms

assessment of client-environment correspondence and discorrespondence

counselor facilitation of actuarially sound decision making by the client

In the paragraphs that follow, emphasis is placed on different problem areas. For additional detail on procedures, the reader may find it useful to consult the previous discussion of counseling process in this book and other texts, such as *A Psychological Theory of Work Adjustment* (Dawis and Lofquist, 1984).

Career Counseling

In career counseling the focus is placed on assisting the client to identify and decide on a career in an occupation or occupational family that corresponds to the client's accurately perceived personality characteristics, or accurate self-image. With respect to timing, the client and counselor would move early on in the counseling process to assess personality and self-image (and its accuracy) in order to establish what capabilities the client will bring to a career and what need-satisfaction the client expects from a career. In this process, client aspirations and ideas about a career will, of course, be addressed.

Accurate client perception of measured personality, then, provides the base against which occupational environment characteristics can be compared in the search for occupations that are correspondent and for which satisfactoriness and satisfaction can be forecast. The process will involve the use of occupational classification systems such as MOCS III and the *Dictionary of Occupational Titles* (DOT). In the decision-making process, the counselor can facilitate appropriate occupational choice by assigning a fairly heavy load of client homework in reality testing, such as the reading of occupational information, consulting outlook information, visiting occupational areas, and interviewing educational authorities and career incumbents. The search and the choice focus on correspondence of person and environment.

Job-Adjustment Counseling

In this kind of counseling the client will likely express dissatisfaction with working conditions, need to change, dissatisfaction with self-performance, burnout, need for midcareer change, or unhappiness with the rewards of the job. Having communicated understanding of the client's presenting problems, the counselor's focus becomes one of determining whether or not the client's self-reports are accurate, are rationalizations, or stem from other client-environment interactions. The timing of approaches in the process dictates early emphasis on obtaining objective descriptive information on the requirement and reinforcer characteristics of the job environment. The process then moves on to assessment of client personality (what the client brings to the job), client understanding of personality (accuracy of client perception and expectations for adjustments), and personality structure in the job situation. The overall focus is on identification of objective correspondences and discorrespondences between client and work environment and counselor interventions to facilitate changed job behavior, more realistic expectations, improved perception of job conditions, or change to a more correspondent job. If the process leads to a focus on counseling for job change, the client and counselor would utilize the procedures discussed for career counseling.

George was irritable at home, seemed to be increasing his drinking, and was losing interest in his work. His family persuaded him to go in for counseling.

George was dissatisfied with his work in accounting and with his supervisor. He reported being passed over for promotion and being criticized frequently. He claimed to have excellent ability with numbers, but biographical information indicated only average success in mathematics-related courses, and more proficiency with spatial problems (especially in his avocational pursuits). His abilities and needs were objectively assessed, and they confirmed the inferences from the biographical data. After extended discussion in interview sessions and some retesting, George decided to explore occupations with lower numerical-ability requirements and higher spatial-ability requirements. With the aid of MOCS III, occupations in the architectural drafting area were identified as promising possibilities. George decided to take training as a drafter and to apply for work as an apprentice in companies employing drafters. Because of financial need, George sought training outside of work hours and continued on his current job. It was easier for him to do that because of his plans for change and because he had a more realistic concept of his abilities. Follow-up showed that George's problems had diminished and that he was more satisfied with his work situation than he had been previously.

This and other case illustrations deal only with one root of discorrespondence. There may be several other reasons in any environment for an individual's lack of satisfaction.

Vocational Rehabilitation Counseling

In vocational rehabilitation counseling the counselor's focus is on assisting the client to return to or to enter work. A first approach might be to determine how much loss or change in abilities and in needs there is in the posttrauma personality compared with the pretrauma personality. (A discussion of this view of disability—as a literal loss—can be found in a monograph by Lofquist et al., 1964.) This approach requires the construction of a pretrauma personality of abilities and needs from prior test data, school records, and pretrauma biographical information, as well as through inference, for example, from the requirement and reinforcer descriptions of previous jobs in which the client was adjusted. Posttrauma personality can then be measured to determine extent of change. It is then necessary to assess the significance of any losses in relation to returning to previous work or similar jobs (looking at fields of work). The counselor will also, of course, get information from physicians and rehabilitation team workers that relates to such matters as physical limitations, planned treatment, training, and environmental restrictions. In exploration for suitable work, the focus is on the fit (correspondence) of the individual client and an occupation, not on what individuals in the client's diagnostic category usually do. Describing the disabling condition of an individual in person-environment-correspondence terms is not the same as describing it in medical diagnostic-category terms.

With medical, team, and pre-post trauma information, client and counselor can work on the client's achieving an accurate self-image and projecting it against descriptive information in occupational classification systems, much as is done in career counseling.

Counseling for Job Change

When the client's presenting problem is the expressed need for job change, the approach is similar to that taken in job-adjustment counseling. The focus is on whether or not change in job would be desirable to achieve work adjustment by redressing significant and irremediable discorrespondences between client personality characteristics and environmental characteristics. The timing of procedures suggests immediate assessment of client personality and self-image and environmental requirements and reinforcers. Client and counselor examine correspondence and determine whether or not significant discorrespondences exist. If they do, information from occupational taxonomies may suggest jobs likely to result in improved P-E fit and consequent adjustment to work.

When reasonable P-E correspondence is found in the present job, attention in counseling may require addressing accuracy of self-image (the perceptual screen through which the client views the environmental characteristics). Attention should also be given to the assessment of client personality style to discover the ways in which the client presents personality structure when interacting with the environment. Counseling for change in personality-style behaviors may improve correspondence with job characteristics to an acceptable level.

Unemployment Counseling

In cases where the client has substantial tenure prior to the current unemployment status, the focus is on generalizing from demonstration of at least minimal satisfactoriness and satisfaction in the previous employment to jobs that are related (i.e., in the same job family and having similar environment characteristics). Use of the information in a classification system such as MOCS III and in the DOT job descriptions will provide appropriate leads for client-counselor discussion and the identification of reemployment potentialities. In cases where the client might be described as "congenitally" (hard-core) unemployed or where previous job history is one of job-hopping across short-term periods of employment, counselor and client would proceed in much the same fashion as in career counseling, with additional client information about discorrespondence experienced in the short-term jobs that did not work out.

Marriage Counseling

The focus here is on viewing the clients—marriage partners or significant others—in terms of their personality structures, self-images, and personality styles in an interaction where each serves as the environment for the other. Assessment of each personality and of how each individual perceives the abilities and needs of the other serving as environment is extremely important. Most important are the achievement of accurate perception of the partner's psychological need structure, and the ability to provide adequate reinforcers for these psychological needs to generate satisfaction. The use of satisfaction questionnaires may provide information about discorrespondences resulting from inadequate reinforcer systems. Correspondences and improved adjustment may be achieved by improving accuracy of perception of the partner's needs and by employing appropriate personality-style actions in the presentation of personality structure.

Jill and Jack lived in a comfortable suburban home, enjoyed an upscale life-style, and were financially very well off, but they found it increasingly hard to communicate with each other. The problem was not sex; they had a satisfying sex life. What appeared to be pulling them apart was a difference in interests. They went to see a counselor.

Though they professed love for each other, Jill and Jack reported less than satisfaction in their marriage. They both took an interest inventory and were surprised to find that they appeared to have similar interests. This made it hard to understand why they did not enjoy their home life together. After some more discussion, the counselor suggested they take a measure of psychological needs. This time they expected to have similar needs and were again surprised because their needs were quite different: one had a high need for social status and the other had a high need for social service. Following test interpretation, the couple reached the point where both understood their own needs and were clear about what reinforcers were and were not important to them. Using individual interviews and, later, joint interviews, the counselor made them aware of each other's needs and helped them to see their differences in preferences for reinforcers and to know what kind of reinforcers were required for each other's satisfaction. They could then reinforce each other and not simply assume that the other person had the same needs they did.

Both Jill and Jack were very satisfied on follow-up.

Family Counseling

Family counseling is even more complex than marriage counseling because of the increased number of individual personalities, self-images, and environments to be considered. It can, however, proceed along the same assumptions as have been stated for marriage counseling. Each family member is treated as an assessable personality in interaction with each other family member serving as an environment. The foci in this kind of counseling are on identifying discorrespondences that are the most significant between particular members of the family unit, and moving through assessment to improved accuracy of self-images, perception of others as environments, and improved reinforcer systems for the principal discorrespondent members. Counseling will probably involve working both with the family unit as a whole and with some members individually when they are central to the problems requiring improved correspondence.

Ellen is a teenager who has developed hostility in family interactions with her parents and older brother. The family cannot understand this, and is devoted to Ellen's having a happy life. The parents have adopted a very laissez-faire policy in their dealings with their children. As a result, Ellen has started drinking with her friends and has gotten into trouble with school authorities. She has shown anger and impatience with teachers and has started to miss some of her classes.

The parents persuaded Ellen to participate in counseling. The counselor had interviews with Ellen, her parents, and her brother separately and together. Over time, the counselor was interested in getting the need structures of the family members (who, along with Ellen, were willing to take the MIQ-G for need assessment). The overly permissive parents and brother were found to have needs similar to Ellen's, except that Ellen had high strength needs in the areas of significant leadership in both the human relations and technical areas, security, and observance of norms and practices.

The counselor worked with the parents and the brother to develop their awareness of Ellen's different need pattern, and of the necessity of their providing norms and supervision of activities to satisfy these different needs. On follow-up with Ellen and her family, the counselor found reduction of hostility and anger and misbehavior on Ellen's part, and an increase in satisfaction with the family situation for both Ellen and the rest of the family.

Retirement Counseling

The purpose of psychological counseling for retirement is the identification of an environment for retirement that will compensate for the client's loss of the work environment. The overall focus is on finding nonwork sets of tasks for which the client has the requisite abilities and in which there are reinforcers like those experienced in work. Client and counselor move first to assess client satisfaction with the reinforcers in the job held prior to retirement, providing there was substantial tenure (implying satisfaction), or in the immediately preceding job family across which there was substantial tenure. From this assessment of satisfaction, client and counselor can infer the pattern of psychological needs the client brings to retirement. The pattern of abilities in the retirement personality can be inferred from the information on minimum ability requirements available for the preretirement occupation(s) in MOCS III. The validity of the inferred need and ability patterns in the personality the client brings to retirement can be tested by using biographical information obtained with a form such as the BIF to forecast needs and abilities.

In the process of identifying nonwork sets of tasks, client and counselor can study job groupings in MOCS III and DOT job descriptions of preretirement jobs for sets of duties that can be performed part-time, paid or unpaid, that could be combined into an overall retirement environment likely to be satisfactory and satisfying—that is, a retirement environment to which the client will be adjusted as he or she was in the case of work. The duties and tasks can be checked for availability against lists typically provided by organizations using volunteers; these can be sought by the client at social agencies, churches, companies, and government agencies for volunteer or part-time "work." The retirement environment composite may involve "work" across more than one environment that is satisfying in its total effect.

The focus in retirement counseling is not just on the client keeping busy, but on finding activities for response and reinforcement that satisfy the retirement personality and fill the large void in psychological satisfaction created by leaving work. For this counseling process to be successful it is necessary for the client to understand the centrality and importance of work to overall life satisfaction, and to subscribe to the philosophy that the best way to retire is to continue to "work."

John retired from a high-level management position very recently and returned yesterday from a vacation. He was going to sleep in this morning and spend a day of relaxation at home. His old habit patterns interfered, however. He arose, dressed as he would for work, had breakfast, and, while drinking his after-breakfast coffee, realized he had no place to go. Someone else was now in his job; he wasn't expected; and, while everyone would be cordial, if he went in as he had for the last twenty years, it would seem strange to his old friends and co-workers, and he would be in the way. John moved to the deck of his comfortable suburban house. He tried to relax with the morning paper and found it depressing when his interests led him to the business section. Two more cups of coffee did not help him identify something worthwhile to do.

John is an achievement-oriented person who likes to solve problems and to see evidence of his accomplishments. He finally decided that it might be productive to get a haircut while he pondered his newly won isolation from the work environment. He did not enjoy himself at the barbershop. His newly acquired peer group was depressing, his lack of people to manage and problems to solve—activity that would challenge his abilities—left him with a strange kind of "postpartum blues" that he had not expected. He knew he would have to find productive activity that would challenge and satisfy him. He wasn't ready simply to enjoy free time.

In counseling, the counselor helped John identify a group of activities that corresponded to his abilities and needs that were correspondent with his work environment during his years in management. The counselor also objectively assessed John's abilities, needs, and interests, and these measurements showed substantive equivalence to levels of the same traits inferred from his biographical history. With the counselor's help, John explored several volunteer activities, such as Little League commissioner, planner and manager of his church's annual festival, managing a fund drive for a local social agency, and the possibility of participating in local politics by managing the campaign of a prospective council member.

Linda retired two years ago from a senior-level position in a large public agency. She had excellent computer skills and liked to work with numbers and budgets. She liked the guidelines, rules, expectations, and demands of her job. She also liked the feeling of accomplishment from completing projects and the recognition she received for doing so. Her management team and co-workers were always there to back her up. Her workdays were full and satisfying, and leisure after work was a pleasant contrast. Now she is on her own, with no outlet for her abilities and little real sense of accomplishment. She misses her friends in the city.

Linda's husband, Carl, will retire next year. His weekends are now fully occupied by work required to maintain the beauty of their property. He cuts grass with his tractor for hours, cuts wood for the fireplace, runs off to the hardware store, does house repairs, and typically dozes off from physical fatigue in the early evening. Linda does not like to garden, sew, can vegetables, or make jelly. She hates cooking. There do not seem to be any home activities that she can enjoy doing. Thinking ahead to a coffee party she had agreed to attend, she knows the conversation will focus on gardening or new recipes, or sewing crafts or the problems and accomplishments of the children. She also knows she will be bored and very quiet. She decides to see a counselor.

In counseling, Linda's needs and abilities are objectively assessed. She compares this objective assessment with the subjective assessment the counselor asked her to make when she first came in. She seemed fairly accurate in her assessment. They move on to an exploration of MOCS III for occupations that would be correspondent and might suggest part-time paid or nonpaid activities that would be satisfying, such as office manager in a health agency clinic, office manager for a small bank, other occupations in banking, church secretary, and part-time supervision in social programs. Now she has something to think about, to plan for, to pursue.

Stress Counseling

The stress counseling discussed here deals with working with clients experiencing psychological stress, not physical or physiological stress. In working with clients expressing feelings of psychological stress and perhaps exhibiting behavioral signs such as anger, anxiety, aggressive action toward the environment, or withdrawal from environmental interaction, the concept of corresponsiveness of individual and environment as a necessary condition for establishing adjustment holds promise for addressing the problem. Corresponsiveness is thought of as a kind of homeostatic mechanism specific to identifiable environments where adjustment is seen as balance. Psychological stress may be defined as an intervening psychological state inferred from antecedent conditions of discorrespondence (imbalance) and consequent behavior directed toward reducing the discorrespondence (reestablishing balance). The indicators of stress (dissatisfaction and unsatisfactoriness in specific environments) are found in consequent behaviors such as those mentioned above (i.e., aggressiveness or withdrawal), which are typically ineffective for resolving the problem. The counseling approach focuses on assessing P-E correspondence for the antecedent conditions, working on improved accuracy of client perception of self and environment if there is a P-E correspondence, and working toward changes in client, environment, or both where a P-E imbalance is found to exist. Examples of imbalance in antecedent conditions might include client skill levels inadequate to meet environment requirements and reinforcer levels well below client reinforcer requirements.

Nho Khanh Du, an Asian-American, has enjoyed continuous employment and has been promoted to a position at the middle-management level. Recently he has been exhibiting behavioral symptoms of stress, such as anger, withdrawal, and anxiety. He admits to his family that he finds several aspects of his working conditions almost unbearable. His wife persuades him to see a physician. The physician rules out physiological reasons for his stress and refers him to a counselor.

The counselor, after assessment of abilities and needs, job reinforcers and ability requirements, finds several discorrespondences that could be made tolerable with some minor adjustments in the workplace. Khanh has not brought his dissatisfactions to the attention of his immediate boss because he was reared in a family that encouraged suppression of dissatisfaction, and because his position is high enough so that in one sense he feels fortunate just to be there. The counselor seeks to correct the antecedent conditions of discorrespondence, the probable cause of Khanh's stress. The counselor works with him to find ways of acting on the environment that would be successful, and helps identify some avocational and social activities that might provide reinforcement not likely to be gained from the job.

Counseling continues so that the effectiveness of the client's newfound activeness can be assessed, and increased client satisfaction and reduction in stress are demonstrated. Khanh has begun to perceive more appropriate reinforcement in work and has become more realistic about what can and cannot be achieved in his situation.

Addiction Counseling

The concepts that underlie P-E-C Theory are useful adjuncts to addiction counseling in that they suggest points of focus for client-counselor attention that should be addressed in the treatment process. The client in addiction counseling is typically there because his or her addiction has resulted in behaviors that are discorrespondent with environmental requirements and are judged to be unsatisfactory and unacceptable by the environments in which the client seeks to achieve and maintain correspondence. A first focal point might well be exploration of kinds of behavior that are unacceptable and the client's views of why the behaviors occurred. Target environments, those with the most problems of discorrespondence, should be identified and the nature of their reinforcement systems described.

Clients in addiction have psychological needs, as do all clients, and self-images that reflect these needs as part of self-perception of personality. A second focal point in counseling is the assessment of the client's needs and of the accuracy of self-image. This will identify the kinds of reinforcers being sought and can lead to discussion of how reinforcement is achieved. In reinforcement terms, addiction may be maintained in at least three ways. First, self-reinforcers may operate. These might involve feelings of achievement, accomplishment, autonomy, creativity, and being in control. In most cases these feelings are delusions, and it is necessary to disabuse the client of their validity, for example, by pointing up realities such as lack of actual accomplishment. Other self-reinforcers stemming from physiological effects of the abused substance — such as hedonistic feelings of pleasure, comfort, safety, and lack of stress — require discussion in terms of their immobilizing effects on permitting satisfactory behaviors that will enable the client to stay in environments and to experience reinforcement of several other important needs. Second, there may be a number of powerful social reinforcers operating to maintain the addiction. Such factors as social status in a group, group conformity, emulation of role models, and camaraderie may maintain the client's unacceptable addictive behavior. This situation points to the need for action on the environment or change in environments. Often in social situations people will reinforce inappropriate behavior by feeling sorry for the individual displaying that behavior.

A third kind of reinforcer may operate in environments where there is institutionalized reinforcement that is not contingent on satisfactory task performance. In some work settings, for example, pay, security, and status may be achieved automatically, without reference to satisfactoriness. In such a case, the environment inadvertently reinforces the addiction.

Counseling for addiction should include assessment of satisfactoriness, analysis of P-E discorrespondence, assessment of psychological needs, and determination of the linkages between reinforcers and social task requirements.

Counseling for Self-Esteem

If a client presents with problems centered around such feelings as low self-esteem, self-denigration, or poor ego strength, the counselor and client may first want to explore whether or not there may be valid bases for low estimation of self-worth. The self-image should be assessed for client estimation of abilities and needs. The resulting profiles should be compared with objective measurements of the same dimensions in the personality. Client and counselor will then likely proceed to work for client achievement of an accurate self-image. Since the client probably judges self on perceived achievements or lack of them in a major environment such as work, environmental requirements and reinforcers should also be assessed. It may be that the client is working under environmental ability requirements considerably below the capabilities suggested by the assessed personality and translates lack of ability utilization or achievement into feelings of lack of actual capability. Environmental change may be in order. The client's personality and the environmental characteristics may fit well (have high correspondence), but the client may not perceive the reinforcers given and may not know that he or she is using abilities well and is achieving. If the client has a self-image that includes estimated low levels of abilities and this proves to be accurate, the counselor may wish to consider a program of skill-enhancement training. Counselor and client may also have discussions of individual differences and the dignity of all individuals at all levels of ability when they perform up to their own individual levels of capacity. The essential worth of jobs at all levels could also be discussed.

P-E-C Theory also has applications for problem solving in business and industry. We have already discussed job-adjustment counseling, and the same procedures can be employed in an employee assistance program setting. In addition, P-E-C approaches can be applied to personnel selection, job transfer, design and redesign of work environments, and employee morale.

Personnel Selection

The focus in the selection of new employees is on identifying individuals who correspond to the particular work environment on the premise that they will be satisfactory and satisfied (i.e., work adjusted) and will stay on the job. Such a focus should ensure continuing productivity and eliminate duplication of selection and training costs for additional new employees.

In preparation for the selection process, the work environments of the target jobs should be described in terms of personality dimensions—that is, in terms of ability requirements and reinforcer patterns. This description is used in addition to the prose description of duties, job classification, and job benefits. Preparation of the description can begin with the listing of skills required to perform job duties and then move to the use of more parsimonious ability dimensions, such as those represented in the GATB. Reinforcer patterns can be identified by using the MJDQ with supervisors and current employees. The resulting psychological job description would resemble those found in MOCS III. Such description of many jobs may, in fact, already be available in MOCS III, with a little adaptation required for use in the particular company setting.

Potential employees can be assessed on the same personality dimensions in the job description and P-E correspondence can be examined to identify the most capable individuals for which satisfactoriness and satisfaction can be predicted. This procedure should increase length of employee tenure and employee morale at the same time it reduces continuing selection costs. Some companies have found it useful to construct a system of classification like MOCS III for all company jobs.

Job Transfer

When job transfer of an employee within the company is being considered, procedures similar to those discussed in the section on job change could be employed. The focus is on improving or maintaining employee performance and need satisfaction (morale) in a new work setting. The job selected for transfer should be one that corresponds to the individual's personality (objectively measured) and self-image (subjectively perceived). It is desirable to assess personality and self-image, determine accuracy of self-image, assess potential transfer jobs, measure employee satisfaction with present job using an instrument such as the MSQ, and identify the most correspondent transfer environment. For optimum P-E fit it may also be desirable to make some changes in the requirements and the reinforcer system in the transfer job that is selected.

Design and Redesign of Work Environments

When new work environments are created, they should be described in work personality terms (i.e., ability requirements and reinforcer systems) to ensure work-environment fit when the employees are selected. It is important to include reinforcement conditions that address a broad range of worker psychological needs. Analysis of how the MIQ needs might be represented may be useful.

When technological changes require the redesign of a work environment, the first concern should be how the new environment will correspond to the personalities (capabilities and needs) of current employees who are to be retained and who will work in the new setting. Group profiles of abilities and needs of the workers in the current environment and a profile of their satisfaction with particular reinforcers in the current environment should permit inferences of what characteristics are necessary or desirable in the restructured work environment. For example, if important reinforcers are no longer present, it may be wise to build in some additional reinforcer conditions to compensate for their loss and to ensure continued employee satisfaction.

Employee Morale

When the morale of a group of employees is judged to be at an undesirable level and results in such behaviors as overt expressions of dissatisfaction, decreases in productivity, increases in production errors, increases in lost time on the job, and increases in accidents, it may be useful to assess the workers' satisfaction with the reinforcer conditions on the job. If a small number of dissatisfied workers are the source of poor morale in the larger group, transfers or dismissals may be required. If dissatisfaction is substantial across the group, attention may need to be given to the inclusion in the work setting of new reinforcers or enhancement of present reinforcers so that they can be readily perceived by most of the group.

Salary Equity Problems

When worker requests for equal pay for comparable work arise, often across jobs, gender, and race, the development of an objective data base should lead to a rational solution to the problem. If satisfactoriness ratings (e.g., on the MSS) are reasonably equal for workers of both genders, or of different races, in the same job, the fairness of comparable pay for being capable of meeting the same job requirements is self-evident. If workers in two or more different jobs maintain that the jobs are comparable and merit equal pay, the satisfactoriness of the workers in the different jobs can be assessed. If the workers are indeed saisfactory in meeting the requirements of the jobs, the job taxon in which each job has membership in a work taxonomy (e.g., MOCS III), by virtue of similarity of job ability requirements and reinforcers, can be located. If two jobs are in the same taxon grouping, equal pay seems reasonable. If the taxa are different, the ability requirements must be compared to determine whether or not significant differences exist for levels of employee task performance. Where significant differences do exist, equal pay may not be merited.

Job Training Programs

When job training programs are legislated to address unemployment problems for untrained workers, attention should be specified in the plans not only for job availability following training, but also for structuring training programs based on assessment of the target jobs for both minimum ability requirements and reinforcer systems. Trainee selection and the training itself should then reflect both the task requirements in performance terms and the reinforcer systems of the target jobs. This is important for transfer of the training experienced to the target jobs to enhance the likelihood of satisfaction, satisfactoriness, and job tenure.

Planning Educational Curricula

In the planning of educational curricula for institutions offering vocational-technical training or specialized professional education (e.g., dentistry, medicine, law, nursing, social work), the construction of the curriculum should begin with assessment data on the characteristics of the target occupations for which workers who will be both satisfactory and satisfied (i.e., adjusted) will be trained. In other words, the curriculum, to be maximally effective, should require and use similar kinds and levels of abilities that characterize the target occupations and should contain similar kinds and levels of reinforcers as the targets. Much of the necessary information on the target occupations is already available in taxonomic form (e.g., in MOCS III).

The kind and manner of delivery of instruction in the educational program can be structured to reflect as closely as possible the target-job situations for which the students are being prepared. Data are not available, however, on educational reinforcer systems. Educational reinforcer patterns (ERPs) for specific curricula can be generated after reinforcer systems reflecting target occupations are built into the curricula, much in the same way that ORPs have been generated. Teachers and satisfactory incumbent students can be used as raters to complete the MEDQ. Procedures for admission of students to these vocational-technical and professional schools should make use of the ability-requirement and reinforcer-system information in the same way as in job selection in industry. The goal of the selection and training is prediction of maximum job adjustment.

Teaching Career Courses

The P-E-C model suggests a number of student projects and discussion topics that may be used in teaching occupational-information and career-planning courses to high school seniors and college freshmen. Instructors may wish to facilitate rational student planning and selection of career areas by assigning the following student experiences:

1. students' estimation of their own standing on ability dimensions and ability classes using an estimation form that includes ability dimensions like those represented in the GATB

2. estimation of psychological need and value classes using a rating rubric that includes a need structure such as the MIQ

3. identification of own measured ability and need/value levels through use of instruments such as the GATB and the MIQ if this is feasible, or by inferring levels from other test scores available in the students' cumulative records

4. completion of the Biographical Information Form for use in estimating actual abilities and needs

5. comparison of estimated and measured levels of abilities and needs; adjustment of self-estimates where there are significant discrepancies; and description of the best appraisal of self-levels of actual abilities and needs to be brought to an occupational environment for interaction with the work environment's requirement and reinforcer system

6. description of the occupational information available and the classification system used in MOCS III

7. comparision of own ability-need pattern with those in MOCS III and location of the ability-need taxa that provide the best personality-environment fit and for which work adjustment (satisfaction and satisfactoriness) can be predicted

8. description of the best-fit occupation(s) and of other information referred to in the taxonomy, such as DOT occupational description, temperaments, interests, and outlook for the occupation(s)

Beginning lecture material should include explanation of basic concepts in P-E-C Theory. Discussion of additional informational sources (e.g., interviews with job incumbents, visits to educational institutions), should also be included.

Chapter 10
Postscript

We hope that this presentation of the P-E-C Theory of Counseling will stimulate a good deal of necessary research to test its propositions, suggest revisions, and generally explicate its concepts. Research is necessary to determine the reliability and validity of the assessment measures that have been included in the Appendix, specifically, the measures of needs, values, reinforcers, and satisfaction, as they relate to environments other than work.

Research should be done on the effectiveness with which satisfaction with other than work environments can be predicted from correspondence using the revised measures. Research is also necessary to determine how subjective P-E correspondence compares with objective P-E correspondence, and to discover the factors associated with differences between the two correspondences.

Studies should be carried out on the effectiveness of counselor or client interventions (structured experiences) on changes in the perception of self (self-image). For example, if clients misjudge their abilities, they could be placed in situations or settings requiring the ability in question, in which the consequences of lack of ability would be clear. Research should ascertain how effective such interventions would be, and with what kinds of clients.

Can you change a person's self-perceptions using certain interventions? What kind of intervention will change the self-image to align with the objective assessment?

Can change in self-image be assessed objectively from such data as repeated client-generated profiles of psychological needs and abilities compared with objective measurements of these traits?

Do increases in client satisfaction, the key to P-E-C counseling, relate positively to the "satisfaction" of the principal people in the target environment? That is, do they find increasing satisfactoriness of the client?

To facilitate counselor assistance to the client of finding more correspondent environments likely to be more satisfying, work should be done on development of reinforcer patterns for kinds of settings and environments other than work—for instance, in marriage, family, social, and educational environments. With this kind of information, it should be possible to develop useful taxonomies modeled after the Minnesota Occupational Classification System III for work-adjustment counseling.

How effective are counselor interview behaviors, verbal and nonverbal reinforcements, in producing change in client self-image? Is the client adjustment process enhanced by counselor adoption of behavior that is optimally correspondent to the client's abilities and needs? In this case, the counselor is seen as the client's main environment in the interviews and as seeking to provide the correct kinds of reinforcers for the client's needs and the ability requirements of which the client is capable. Examples might include verbal communication at the appropriate client ability level, and allowing an autonomous client substantial freedom in making decisions in the counseling process.

Does counseling that results in increased correspondence with environments and increased client satisfaction result in maximizing utilization of the client's abilities? That is, do such changes result in client growth? Research should also determine whether or not improved perception of objective psychological needs and abilities (more accurate self-image) results in client growth.

The preceding suggestions describe an ambitious but necessary basic research program to establish and test the usefulness of the P-E-C Theory of Counseling across a variety of environments. Additional research is suggested in the propositions and corollaries presented in the formal statement of the theory in Chapter 4.

Appendix

Reproduced from the original instruments

Biographical Information Form
Vocational Assessment Clinic

This form is designed to obtain information about your personal history that will
be useful in vocational assessment. It consists of three parts: Part I asks
about your educational history, work history, and vocationally related activities;
Part II asks for information about your childhood and adolescent years; and
Part III asks about your present situation. (Use the back of this page for additional
information that does not fit in the space given).

Part I

Section A: Educational History

1. How many years of school have you finished?

_____ less than high school graduate

_____ high school graduate

_____ voc/tech school graduate

_____ some college

_____ college graduate

_____ some graduate work or professional school

_____ graduate or professional degree

2. Rank the following types of courses putting first (Rank 1) that area in which
    you had the most courses in junior high school and/or high school, and putting
    last (Rank 5) that area in which you had the fewest courses.

Business	1.	_____
Math	2.	_____
Science	3.	_____
Shop/Technical	4.	_____
Social Studies	5.	_____

3. List and describe below job-related training and/or education you have had
    beyond high school training. (This would include any trade school, college
    or university, vocational-technical or business school, correspondence,
    extension or special courses or programs, apprenticeship or service school.)

Where Taken	Dates	Course Program or Major Area of Study	Degree or Certification
_____	___to___	_____	_____
_____	___to___	_____	_____
_____	___to___	_____	_____
_____	___to___	_____	_____
_____	___to___	_____	_____
_____	___to___	_____	_____

-2-

4. Have you taken any independent study/reading courses? ☐ yes ☐ no

    If yes, how many? _____

5. List any self-improvement courses you have taken (e.g., human relations, assertiveness training, Dale Carnegie, speed reading, how-to-study).

    _____

    _____

Section B: Work History

1. At what age did you start working regularly for pay? _____

             ☐ part-time   ☐ full-time?

2. How many different jobs have you had in the last five years? _____

3. List and describe below and on the following page your last five jobs beginning with your current or most recent job. (Do not include military service.)

    Job Title _____

    Employer/Address _____

    Dates: _____to_____ Pay per month $ _____ Hours per week _____

    Describe what you do (did) on this job _____

    _____

    How do (did) you like this job? (Check one)

        ☐ I hate(d) it   ☐ I like(d) it

        ☐ I dislike(d) it   ☐ I am (was) enthusiastic about it

        ☐ I don't (didn't) like it   ☐ I love(d) it

        ☐ I am (was) indifferent to it

    Job Title _____

    Employer/Address _____

    Dates: _____to_____ Pay per month $ _____ Hours per week _____

    Describe what you did on this job _____

    _____

    Did you like this job? (Check one)

                    ☐ I liked it

                    ☐ it was okay

                    ☐ I mostly didn't like it

-3-

Job Title _____

Employer/Address _____

Dates: _____to_____   Pay per month $_____   Hours per week _____

Describe what you did on this job _____

_____

Did you like this job? (Check one)

[ ] I liked it

[ ] it was okay

[ ] I mostly didn't like it

Job Title _____

Employer/Address _____

Dates: _____to_____   Pay per month $_____   Hours per week _____

Describe what you did on this job _____

_____

Did you like this job? (Check one)

[ ] I liked it

[ ] it was okay

[ ] I mostly didn't like it

Job Title _____

Employer/Address _____

Dates: _____to_____   Pay per month $_____   Hours per week _____

Describe what you did on this job _____

_____

Did you like this job? (Check one)

[ ] I liked it

[ ] it was okay

[ ] I mostly didn't like it

4. Which one of the jobs on the preceding pages did you hold for the longest period of time? _____

5. Which one of the jobs did you like best? _____

-4-

6. If these jobs (longest and liked best) are the same, only check the boxes under longest. If these jobs are not the same, check the boxes on the left for the job you held the longest and the boxes on the right for the job you liked best.

	Longest	Liked Best
Did you see the finished product of your work?	☐ yes	☐ yes
	☐ sometimes	☐ sometimes
	☐ no	☐ no
Did you supervise others?	☐ yes	☐ yes
	☐ no	☐ no
Did you develop projects that others completed?	☐ yes	☐ yes
	☐ no	☐ no
Did you receive praise from your supervisor for a job well done?	☐ yes	☐ yes
	☐ no	☐ no
How much time did you spend outdoors?	☐ most or all	☐ most or all
	☐ about half	☐ about half
	☐ little or none	☐ little or none
Did you have much free time on the job?	☐ yes	☐ yes
	☐ sometimes	☐ sometimes
	☐ no	☐ no
How did you work most of the time?	☐ alone	☐ alone
	☐ with a few people	☐ with a few people
	☐ with many people	☐ with many people
How were you supervised?	☐ supervised most of the time	☐ supervised most of the time
	☐ not supervised most of the time	☐ not supervised most of the time
Who set your work routine?	☐ followed a set routine, paced for you	☐ followed a set routine, paced for you
	☐ operated within a loose routine, paced yourself	☐ operated within a loose routine, paced yourself
	☐ established your own routine and pacing	☐ established your own routine and pacing

-5-

7. Have you ever:

created or redesigned your own job? ☐ yes ☐ no

suggested changes in company policy or practice? ☐ yes ☐ no

asked for a raise in pay? ☐ yes ☐ no

refused to do a task required by your job? ☐ yes ☐ no

put off doing tasks required by your job until you didn't have to do them? ☐ yes ☐ no

changed work methods in your job? ☐ yes ☐ no

8. For each of the following work tasks, check one of the boxes (seldom, sometimes, or frequently) for the job you held the longest; then check one of the boxes for the job you liked best. If these jobs are the same, check only the boxes under longest.

	Longest			Liked Best		
	Seldom	Some-times	Freq-uently	Seldom	Some-times	Freq-uently
Working with numbers	☐	☐	☐	☐	☐	☐
Working with words, ideas	☐	☐	☐	☐	☐	☐
Working with forms, patterns, graphs	☐	☐	☐	☐	☐	☐
Advising or counseling others	☐	☐	☐	☐	☐	☐
Waiting on people	☐	☐	☐	☐	☐	☐
Teaching or supervising	☐	☐	☐	☐	☐	☐
Speaking to or communicating with others	☐	☐	☐	☐	☐	☐
Selling or entertaining	☐	☐	☐	☐	☐	☐
Placing or moving large objects	☐	☐	☐	☐	☐	☐
Driving or steering equipment	☐	☐	☐	☐	☐	☐
Handling small objects, use of fingers (like typing)	☐	☐	☐	☐	☐	☐
Observing or tending things or machines	☐	☐	☐	☐	☐	☐

-6-

9. How many jobs have you obtained:

through friends or family? _____

through a placement or employment agency? _____

through being contacted by the company? _____

through want ads or applying in person? _____

10. Were you ever in the military service? ☐ yes ☐ no

If yes: What branch? _____

How long? _____ years

Rank at entry? _____

Rank at discharge? _____

Awards? (List) _____

Did you receive any occupational training? ☐ yes ☐ no

If yes, for what occupation(s)? _____

Type of discharge _____

How did you feel about the military service?

☐ I liked it   ☐ it was okay   ☐ I mostly didn't like it

Section C: Related Activities

1. For each of the following general kinds of activities check one of the boxes
(seldom, sometimes, or frequently) that best describes how much you were
involved in that kind of activity in the last five years.

	seldom or not at all	sometimes	frequently
Team sports like basketball or hockey	☐	☐	☐
Fixing things, working on cars	☐	☐	☐
Eating out	☐	☐	☐
Activities like model building or watch repair	☐	☐	☐
Individual sports like skiing, bowling	☐	☐	☐
Walking or jogging	☐	☐	☐
Self-improvement activities like physical fitness, yoga	☐	☐	☐
Driving around	☐	☐	☐
Outdoor activities (other than sports)	☐	☐	☐

-7-

	seldom or not at all	sometimes	frequently
Attending art galleries, concerts, plays	☐	☐	☐
Home carpentry, repairs or painting	☐	☐	☐
Watching television, weekly serials or sports	☐	☐	☐
Watching plays, documentaries, educational TV	☐	☐	☐
Playing musical instruments or singing	☐	☐	☐
Composing music, writing stories, designing	☐	☐	☐
Craft activities like knitting, leatherwork	☐	☐	☐
Games like pool, pinball or cards	☐	☐	☐
Listening to music	☐	☐	☐
Going to the movies	☐	☐	☐
Housework or household activities	☐	☐	☐
Activities like carving or composing photographs	☐	☐	☐
Attending sports events, drag races	☐	☐	☐
Going to taverns or bars	☐	☐	☐
Reading best sellers	☐	☐	☐
Playing bingo, games of chance	☐	☐	☐
Reading classical literature or history	☐	☐	☐
Stamp collecting or working crossword puzzles	☐	☐	☐
Reading community newspapers, magazines like McCall's	☐	☐	☐
Reading books, reports, manuals that relate to your job	☐	☐	☐
Reading newspapers and magazines like Time, Newsweek	☐	☐	☐
Writing letters to newspapers, city hall, Congressman	☐	☐	☐

2. List the awards or prizes you have received for things you have done.

_____

-8-

3. What kinds of organizations or clubs have you been a member of in the <u>past five years</u>? What offices or active committee memberships have you held?

Community organizations: (name/office held) _____

_____

Church or religious organizations: (name/office held) _____

_____

Hobby, interest, or study groups: (name/office held) _____

_____

Political organizations: (name/office held) _____

_____

Social organizations: (name/office held) _____

_____

Business, trade, labor union, or professional organizations: (name/office held)

_____

4. Do you have any health problems that limit your activities? ☐ yes ☐ no

5. How many times in the last five years have you been hospitalized for longer than a week? (Do not count hospitalizations for check ups.) _____

6. How many houses or apartments have you lived in in the last five years? _____

Part II

The questions in this part of the form are about <u>the time period before you were 18 years old</u>. Answer the questions with that time period in mind.

1. How many adults did you typically live with? _____

2. How many people younger than you did you typically live with? _____

3. How many years did you live on a farm? _____ in a small town or city (less than 100,000)? _____ in a large city? _____

4. Number of different communities or cities you lived in _____

5. Number of different residences you lived in (count each address, including apartment houses) _____

6. Did you leave home before age 18? ☐ yes ☐ no

7. What work did you do for pay during this period? (Check all that apply)

___ babysitting   ___ store clerk

___ paper route   ___ farm work, laborer

___ busperson,   ___ other (name them) _____
    waiter/waitress

-9-

8. How did you spend your free time outside work or school?

☐ mostly alone

☐ mostly with one or two friends

☐ mostly in groups of three or more

9. Did you have any health problems that restricted your activities?

☐ yes ☐ no   If yes, what were these? _____

_____

10. How many times were you hospitalized for longer than a week? (Do not count hospitalizations for check-ups.) _____

11. Did you attend public school? ☐ yes ☐ no If yes, how many years? _____

12. Did you attend private or parochial schools? ☐ yes ☐ no
    If yes, for how many years? _____

13. In school did you break the rules? (Check one)

☐ never   ☐ sometimes

☐ almost never   ☐ frequently

14. In school were you punished for breaking the rules? (Check one)

☐ never   ☐ sometimes

☐ almost never   ☐ frequently

15. For each of the following activities check one of the boxes (seldom, sometimes, or frequently) that best describes how much you were into that kind of activity.

	seldom or not at all	sometimes	frequently
Art work or craft activities	☐	☐	☐
Building or fixing things	☐	☐	☐
Community activities, organizations	☐	☐	☐
Dancing	☐	☐	☐
Extra-curricular school activities	☐	☐	☐
Going to concerts	☐	☐	☐
Going to the movies	☐	☐	☐
Hanging around	☐	☐	☐

-10-

	seldom or not at all	sometimes	frequently
Housework or household tasks	☐	☐	☐
Listening to music	☐	☐	☐
Outdoor activities other than sports	☐	☐	☐
Playing musical instruments or singing	☐	☐	☐
Reading	☐	☐	☐
Sports	☐	☐	☐
Television	☐	☐	☐
Time with friends	☐	☐	☐
Working	☐	☐	☐

16. Were you happy with your life during this period of time? (Check one)

☐ yes   ☐ somewhat   ☐ no

Part III

The following questions are about your present situation.

1. How many people do you live with now? _____
2. How many are over the age of 16? _____
3. How many times have you been married? _____
4. If you are currently married, how long have you been married? _____ years
5. Spouse's age _____, years of education _____, occupation _____
6. Father's age _____, years of education _____, occupation _____
7. Mother's age _____, years of education _____, occupation _____
8. List your brothers' and sisters' ages, years of education, and occupation.

	Age	Yrs. of Ed.	Occupation
Brothers	_____	_____	_____
	_____	_____	_____
	_____	_____	_____
Sisters	_____	_____	_____
	_____	_____	_____
	_____	_____	_____

-11-

9. List your children's ages, sex, years of education, and occupation (if any).

Age	Sex	Yrs. of Ed.	Occupation
___	___	_____	_____
___	___	_____	_____
___	___	_____	_____
___	___	_____	_____

10. How many people do you see <u>socially</u> outside work on a weekly basis? _____

11. How many of them are from a higher income level? _____

12. How many of them are from a lower income level? _____

13. Of the people you see weekly, how many do you know through work? _____

14. In your home who makes the decisions about paying bills? (Check one only)

    ☐ yourself   ☐ other person

    ☐ you and other person   ☐ not relevant to you

15. Who makes decisions about caring for or disciplining the children? (Check one only)

    ☐ yourself   ☐ other person

    ☐ you and other person   ☐ not relevant to you

16. Who makes decisions about what you do for fun or entertainment? (Check one only)

    ☐ yourself   ☐ other person

    ☐ you and other person   ☐ not relevant to you

17. Do you keep a budget and account of your spending? (Check one)

    ☐ keep exact records and follow a budget

    ☐ keep records and manage according to a general plan

    ☐ never budget or keep records

18. Do you know how much retirement income you will have? (Check one)

    ☐ yes, exactly

    ☐ yes, generally

    ☐ no

-12-

19. How much life insurance do you have? (Check one)

☐ none

☐ less than three times my yearly earnings

☐ three times my yearly earnings or more

☐ don't really know

20. How many dependents other than yourself do you support? _____

21. In a typical week, how much time do you spend:

	none or a few hours	5 to 10 hours	10 to 20 hours	over 20 hours
Working (including work in the home, also transportation to and from work)	☐	☐	☐	☐
Personal activities like dressing, grooming, and eating	☐	☐	☐	☐
Television	☐	☐	☐	☐
Organization activities	☐	☐	☐	☐
Time with people in your home	☐	☐	☐	☐
Time with people from outside your home	☐	☐	☐	☐
Physical exercise	☐	☐	☐	☐
Hobbies or interest activities	☐	☐	☐	☐
Attending classes and doing class homework	☐	☐	☐	☐
Reading (other than for school)	☐	☐	☐	☐
Other (please describe):				
_____	☐	☐	☐	☐
_____	☐	☐	☐	☐

Thank you for your cooperation and patience in
filling out this form.

Do not write on this booklet

MINNESOTA

IMPORTANCE QUESTIONNAIRE

GENERAL

TRIAD FORM

Vocational Psychology Research

UNIVERSITY OF MINNESOTA

DIRECTIONS

The purpose of this questionnaire is to find out what you consider **important** in your **target environment**, the kind of job you would most like to have.

On the following pages you will find statements about work. The statements are in groups of three.

· Read each group of statements carefully.
· Decide which statement of the three is the **most important** to you in your **target environment**. Mark your choice on the answer sheet.
· Then decide which statement of the three is the **least important** to you in your **target environment**. This statement must be different from the statement that is most important to you. Mark your choice on the answer sheet.

Do not mark in this booklet. Directions on how to mark the answer sheet are given below.

Do this for all groups of statements. Work as rapidly as you can. Read each group of statements, mark your choices, then move on to the next group of statements. Be sure to choose **both** a **most important** and a **least important** statement in each group. Do not go back to change your answers for any group of statements.

Remember: For each group of statements you are to decide which of the three statements is the **most important** to you on your **target environment** and which is the **least important** to you on you **target environment**. Mark your choices on the answer sheet, not on this booklet.

HOW TO MARK THE ANSWER SHEET

First

Print your name in the space provided and fill in the other information requested.

To fill in the answer sheet

Start with item 1.

Item 1 is the first group of three statements on page 1 of this questionnnaire.

On the answer sheet for item 1 there are two groups of three circles, as shown in the example below:

```
          Most Important   Least Important
     1.     a   b   c   |   a   b   c
```

The three circles on the left are for the statement that is most important to you. The three circles on the right are for the statement that is **least important** to you. The statement that is most important to you must be different from the statement that is least important to you.

A circle with an "a" in it stands for statement "a". A circle with a "b" in it stands for statement "b". A circle with a "c" in it stands for statement "c".

For the three circles on the **left** fill in the circle that stands for the statement that is **most important** to you. For the three circles on the **right** fill in the circle that stands for the statement that is **least important** to you.

Here are two examples:

Suppose that statement "a" is the most important to you and statement "b" is the least important, you would fill in the answer sheet as shown below:

Most Important Least Important
1.   a   b   c | a   b   c

Suppose that statement "c" is the most important to you and statement "a" is the least important, you would fill in the answer sheet as shown below:

Most Important Least Important
1.   a   b   c | a   b   c

You must fill in only two answers for each numbered group of three statements, and the statement that you choose as most important must be different from the statement that you choose as least important.

Do this for each numbered group of three statements.

Remember, do not mark your answers on this booklet. Use the answer sheet.

Page 1

Ask yourself: Which is the **most important** to me in my **target environment**?

Then ask yourself: Which is the **least important** to me in my **target environment**?

1. a. I could tell people what to do.
       OR
   b. People in my group would be easy to make friends with.
       OR
   c. The group would provide for my continuing membership.

2. a. My group leader would communicate expectations well.
       OR
   b. My rewards would compare well with those of others.
       OR
   c. The norms and practices would be observed consistently.

3. a. I could get a feeling of accomplishment.
       OR
   b. I could try out my own ideas.
       OR
   c. I could get recognition for the things I do.

4. a. I could do things alone.
       OR
   b. I could do things for other people.
       OR
   c. I could be "somebody" in the group.

5. a. I could do things without feeling they are morally wrong.
       OR
   b. I could plan things independently
       OR
   c. My group leader would back me up.

6. a. I could make decisions on my own.
       OR
   b. I could do something that makes use of my abilities.
       OR
   c. I could do something different every day.

7. a. I could have good operating conditions.
       OR
   b. I could have an opportunity for self-advancement.
       OR
   c. I could be busy all the time.

Page 2

Ask yourself: Which is the **most important** to me in my **target environment**?

Then ask yourself: Which is the **least important** to me in my **target environment**?

8. a. I could get a feeling of accomplishment.
    OR
    b. I could tell people what to do.
    OR
    c. I could do things without feeling they are morally wrong.

9. a. I could do something different every day.
    OR
    b. I could get recognition for the things I do.
    OR
    c. My rewards would compare well with those of others.

10. a. I could do something that makes use of my abilities.
    OR
    b. I could have an opportunity for self-advancement.
    OR
    c. I could do things for other people.

11. a. I could have good operating conditions.
    OR
    b. My group leader would back me up.
    OR
    c. The norms and practices would be observed consistently.

12. a. I could make decisions on my own.
    OR
    b. People in my group would be easy to make friends with.
    OR
    c. My group leader would communicate expectations well.

13. a. I could try out my own ideas.
    OR
    b. I could be busy all the time.
    OR
    c. I could be "somebody" in the group.

14. a. The group would provide for my continuing membership.
    OR
    b. I could do things alone.
    OR
    c. I could plan things independently

Page 3

Ask yourself: Which is the **most important** to me in my **target environment**?

Then ask yourself: Which is the **least important** to me in my **target environment**?

15. a. I could do things for other people.
    OR
    b. My rewards would compare well with those of others.
    OR
    c. I could tell people what to do.

16. a. I could do things without feeling they are morally wrong.
    OR
    b. I could make decisions on my own.
    OR
    c. I could be "somebody" in the group.

17. a. I could plan things independently
    OR
    b. My group leader would communicate expectations well.
    OR
    c. I could have an opportunity for self-advancement.

18. a. The group would provide for my continuing membership.
    OR
    b. I could do something different every day.
    OR
    c. I could be busy all the time.

19. a. I could get recognition for the things I do.
    OR
    b. I could have good operating conditions.
    OR
    c. I could do something that makes use of my abilities.

20. a. My group leader would back me up.
    OR
    b. I could do things alone.
    OR
    c. I could try out my own ideas.

21. a. The norms and practices would be observed consistently.
    OR
    b. I could get a feeling of accomplishment.
    OR
    c. People in my group would be easy to make friends with.

Page 4

Ask yourself: Which is the **most important** to me in my **target environment?**

Then ask yourself: Which is the **least important** to me in my **target environment?**

22. a. I could get recognition for the things I do.
    OR
    b. I could plan things independently
    OR
    c. I could make decisions on my own.

23. a. I could try out my own ideas.
    OR
    b. I could do things for other people.
    OR
    c. My group leader would communicate expectations well.

24. a. People in my group would be easy to make friends with.
    OR
    b. I could be "somebody" in the group.
    OR
    c. I could have good operating conditions.

25. a. I could do things alone.
    OR
    b. The norms and practices would be observed consistently.
    OR
    c. I could do something different every day.

26. a. I could do things without feeling they are morally wrong.
    OR
    b. I could be busy all the time.
    OR
    c. My rewards would compare well with those of others.

27. a. I could get a feeling of accomplishment.
    OR
    b. I could have an opportunity for self-advancement.
    OR
    c. The group would provide for my continuing membership.

28. a. My group leader would back me up.
    OR
    b. I could tell people what to do.
    OR
    c. I could do something that makes use of my abilities.

Page 5

Ask yourself: Which is the **most important** to me in my **target** environment?

Then ask yourself: Which is the **least important** to me in my **target** environment?

29. a. I could do something different every day.
    OR
    b. I could have good operating conditions.
    OR
    c. I could plan things independently

30. a. I could have an opportunity for self-advancement.
    OR
    b. I could tell people what to do.
    OR
    c. The norms and practices would be observed consistently.

31. a. I could do things alone.
    OR
    b. I could do things without feeling they are morally wrong.
    OR
    c. I could get recognition for the things I do.

32. a. My rewards would compare well with those of others.
    OR
    b. People in my group would be easy to make friends with.
    OR
    c. I could try out my own ideas.

33. a. I could make decisions on my own.
    OR
    b. The group would provide for my continuing membership.
    OR
    c. I could do things for other people.

34. a. I could do something that makes use of my abilities
    OR
    b. I could get a feeling of accomplishment.
    OR
    c. I could be busy all the time.

35. a. I could be "somebody" in the group.
    OR
    b. My group leader would back me up.
    OR
    c. My group leader would communicate expectations well.

Page 6

Ask yourself: Which is the **most important** to me in my **target environment**?

Then ask yourself: Which is the **least important** to me in my **target environment**?

36. a. I could have an opportunity for self-advancement.
     OR
     b. I could try out my own ideas.
     OR
     c. I could make decisions on my own.

37. a. I could have good operating conditions.
     OR
     b. I could get a feeling of accomplishment.
     OR
     c. I could do things alone.

38. a. My rewards would compare well with those of others.
     OR
     b. The group would provide for my continuing membership.
     OR
     c. My group leader would back me up.

39. a. My group leader would communicate expectations well.
     OR
     b. I could do things without feeling they are morally wrong.
     OR
     c. I could do something that makes use of my abilities.

40. a. The norms and practices would be observed consistently.
     OR
     b. I could be "somebody" in the group.
     OR
     c. I could plan things independently

41. a. I could do things for other people.
     OR
     b. I could do something different every day.
     OR
     c. People in my group would be easy to make friends with.

42. a. I could be busy all the time.
     OR
     b. I could tell people what to do.
     OR
     c. I could get recognition for the things I do.

Page 7

Ask yourself: Which is the **most important** to me in my **target environment**?

Then ask yourself: Which is the **least important** to me in my **target environment**?

43. a. I could be "somebody" in the group.
    OR
    b. The group would provide for my continuing membership.
    OR
    c. I could do something that makes use of my abilities.

44. a. People in my group would be easy to make friends with.
    OR
    b. I could get recognition for the things I do.
    OR
    c. My group leader would back me up.

45. a. I could be busy all the time.
    OR
    b. The norms and practices would be observed consistently.
    OR
    c. I could make decisions on my own.

46. a. I could plan things independently
    OR
    b. I could do things for other people.
    OR
    c. I could get a feeling of accomplishment.

47. a. I could have an opportunity for self-advancement.
    OR
    b. My rewards would compare well with those of others.
    OR
    c. I could do things alone.

48. a. I could have good operating conditions.
    OR
    b. My group leader would communicate expectations well.
    OR
    c. I could tell people what to do.

49. a. I could try out my own ideas.
    OR
    b. I could do something different every day.
    OR
    c. I could do things without feeling they are morally wrong.

Page 8

Ask yourself: Which is the **most important** to me in my **target environment?**

Then ask yourself: Which is the **least important** to me in my **target environment?**

50. a. I could do things for other people.
    OR
    b. I could be busy all the time.
    OR
    c. My group leader would back me up.

51. a. People in my group would be easy to make friends with.
    OR
    b. I could do something that makes use of my abilities.
    OR
    c. I could do things alone.

52. a. I could do something different every day.
    OR
    b. My group leader would communicate expectations well.
    OR
    c. I could get a feeling of accomplishment.

53. a. I could be "somebody" in the group.
    OR
    b. I could get recognition for the things I do.
    OR
    c. I could have an opportunity for self-advancement.

54. a. I could tell people what to do.
    OR
    b. I could plan things independently
    OR
    c. I could try out my own ideas.

55. a. The norms and practices would be observed consistently.
    OR
    b. I could do things without feeling they are morally wrong.
    OR
    c. The group would provide for my continuing membership.

56. a. My rewards would compare well with those of others.
    OR
    b. I could make decisions on my own.
    OR
    c. I could have good operating conditions.

Page 9

Ask yourself: Which is the **most important** to me in my **target environment**?

Then ask yourself: Which is the **least important** to me in my **target environment**?

57. a. I could do something that makes use of my abilities.
    OR
    b. The norms and practices would be observed consistently.
    OR
    c. I could try out my own ideas.

58. a. I could be busy all the time.
    OR
    b. I could plan things independently
    OR
    c. People in my group would be easy to make friends with.

59. a. I could get a feeling of accomplishment.
    OR
    b. I could be "somebody" in the group.
    OR
    c. My rewards would compare well with those of others.

60. a. I could make decisions on my own.
    OR
    b. I could do things alone.
    OR
    c. I could tell people what to do.

61. a. I could do something different every day.
    OR
    b. My group leader would back me up.
    OR
    c. I could have an opportunity for self-advancement.

62. a. I could get recognition for the things I do.
    OR
    b. The group would provide for my continuing membership.
    OR
    c. My group leader would communicate expectations well.

63. a. I could do things without feeling they are morally wrong.
    OR
    b. I could have good operating conditions.
    OR
    c. I could do things for other people.

Page 10

Ask yourself: Which is the **most important** to me in my **target environment**?

Then ask yourself: Which is the **least important** to me in my **target environment**?

64. a. My group leader would communicate expectations well.
         OR
     b. I could do things alone.
         OR
     c. I could be busy all the time.

65. a. The group would provide for my continuing membership.
         OR
     b. I could try out my own ideas.
         OR
     c. I could have good operating conditions.

66. a. I could tell people what to do.
         OR
     b. I could be "somebody" in the group.
         OR
     c. I could do something different every day.

67. a. The norms and practices would be observed consistently.
         OR
     b. I could get recognition for the things I do.
         OR
     c. I could do things for other people.

68. a. My group leader would back me up.
         OR
     b. I could make decisions on my own.
         OR
     c. I could get a feeling of accomplishment.

69. a. I could plan things independently
         OR
     b. I could do something that makes use of my abilities.
         OR
     c. My rewards would compare well with those of others.

70. a. I could have an opportunity for self-advancement.
         OR
     b. People in my group would be easy to make friends with.
         OR
     c. I could do things without feeling they are morally wrong.

Page 11

On this page consider each statement and decide whether or not it is important to have in your target environment.

If you think that the statement is **important** for your **target environment**, fill in the circle in the "**Yes**" column of your answer sheet.

If you think that the statement is **not important** for your **target environment**, fill in the circle in the "**No**" column of your answer sheet.

In my **target environment** it is important that . . .

71. I could do something that makes use of my abilities.

72. I could get a feeling of accomplishment.

73. I could be busy all the time.

74. I could have an opportunity for self-advancement.

75. I could tell people what to do.

76. The norms and practices would be observed consistently.

77. My rewards would compare well with those of others.

78. People in my group would be easy to make friends with.

79. I could try out my own ideas.

80. I could do things alone.

81. I could do things without feeling they are morally wrong.

82. I could get recognition for the things I do.

83. I could make decisions on my own.

84. The group would provide for my continuing membership.

85. I could do things for other people.

86. I could be "somebody" in the group.

87. My group leader would back me up.

88. My group leader would communicate expectations well.

89. I could do something different every day.

90. I could have good operating conditions.

91. I could plan things independently.

Now please check your answer sheet

For items 1 to 70, make sure that:

- you have filled in only one circle for the statement most important to you.

- you have filled in only one circle for the statement least important to you.

- the statement you have filled in as most important is different from the statement you have filled in as least important.

For items 71 to 91, make sure that:

- you have filled in only one circle.

Then bring your answer sheet and questionnaire to the person who gave you this booklet.

MINNESOTA ENVIRONMENT

DESCRIPTION QUESTIONNAIRE

Confidential   For Research Purposes Only

On the following pages you are asked to rank statements
on the basis of how well they describe the environment of:

_____

Statements about this environment are in groups of five. You are asked to consider
each group of five individually and rank the five statements in terms of how well they
describe the environment, using the numbers "1" to "5". Then go to the next group of five
statements and make the same kind of ranking.

For example, your answers on a group of statements might look like this:

People in this environment...
  4 get full credit for what they do.
  3 are of service to other people.
  1 have freedom to use their own judgment.
  5 do new and original things on their own.
  2 have the chance to get ahead.

This means that, of the five statements, you consider "have freedom to use their own
judgment" as most descriptive of the environment; "have the chance to get ahead" as the
next most descriptive statement; and so on.

You will find some of these comparisons more difficult to make than others, but it is
important that you rank every statement in each group.

All information will be held in strictest confidence.

VOCATIONAL PSYCHOLOGY RESEARCH

UNIVERSITY OF MINNESOTA

Code Number

_ _ _ _ _ _ _ _

Please rank the five statements in each group on the basis of how well they describe the environment mentioned on the front page. Write a "1" by the statement that best describes the environment; write a "2" by the statement that provides the next best description; continue ranking all five statements, using a "5" for the statement that describes the environment least well.

People in this environment...
_____are busy all the time.
_____do things for other people.
_____try out their own ideas.
_____are rewarded well in comparison with others.
_____have opportunities for self-advancement.

People in this environment...
_____do things for other people.
_____have something different to do every day.
_____get a feeling of accomplishment.
_____have group leaders who communicate expectations well.
_____have norms and practices that are observed consistently.

People in this environment...
_____do things without feeling that they are morally wrong.
_____have group leaders who back them up.
_____have something different to do every day.
_____make use of their individual abilities.
_____are busy all the time.

People in this environment...
_____have norms and practices that are observed consistently.
_____try out their own ideas.
_____make use of their individual abilities.
_____are easy to make friends with.
_____have the position of "somebody" in the group.

People in this environment...
_____have group leaders who communicate expectations well.
_____plan their activities with little supervision.
_____have group leaders who back them up.
_____try out their own ideas.
_____have good operating conditions.

Please rank the five statements in each group on the basis of how well they describe the environment mentioned on the front page. Write a "1" by the statement that best describes the environment; write a "2" by the statement that provides the next best description; continue ranking all five statements, using a "5" for the statement that describes the environment least well.

People in this environment...
_____receive recognition for the things they do.
_____do things without feeling that they are morally wrong.
_____plan their activities with little supervision.
_____do things for other people.
_____are easy to make friends with.

People in this environment...
_____have group leaders who back them up.
_____have norms and practices that are observed consistently.
_____are rewarded well in comparison with others.
_____receive recognition for the things they do.
_____tell other people what to do.

People in this environment...
_____have something different to do every day.
_____are easy to make friends with.
_____make decisions on their own.
_____have good operating conditions.
_____are rewarded well in comparison with others.

People in this environment...
_____make use of their individual abilities.
_____tell other people what to do.
_____have good operating conditions.
_____have assurance of continuing participation.
_____do things for other people.

People in this environment...
_____make decisions on their own.
_____are busy all the time.
_____have assurance of continuing participation
_____have norms and practices that are observed consistently.
_____plan their activities with little supervision.

Please rank the five statements in each group on the basis of how well they describe the environment mentioned on the front page. Write a "1" by the statement that best describes the environment; write a "2" by the statement that provides the next best description; continue ranking all five statements, using a "5" for the statement that describes the environment least well.

_____

People in this environment...
_____get a feeling of accomplishment.
_____make decisions on their own.
_____tell other people what to do.
_____do things without feeling that they are morally wrong.
_____try out their own ideas.
_____

People in this environment...
_____are easy to make friends with.
_____have assurance of continuing participation.
_____have opportunities for self advancement.
_____have group leaders who back them up.
_____get a feeling of accomplishment.
_____

People in this environment...
_____plan their activities with little supervision.
_____have opportunities for self-advancement.
_____have the position of "somebody" in the group.
_____tell other people what to do.
_____have something different to do every day.
_____

People in this environment...
_____are rewarded well in comparison with others.
_____get a feeling of accomplishment.
_____do things alone.
_____plan their activities with little supervision.
_____make use of their individual abilities.
_____

People in this environment...
_____tell other people what to do.
_____have group leaders who communicate expectations well.
_____are easy to make friends with.
_____are busy all the time.
_____do things alone.
_____

Please rank the five statements in each group on the basis of how well they describe the environment mentioned on the front page. Write a "1" by the statement that best describes the environment; write a "2" by the statement that provides the next best description; continue ranking all five statements, using a "5" for the statement that describes the environment least well.

People in this environment...

_____have assurance of continuing participation.
_____are rewarded well in comparison with others.
_____have group leaders who communicate expectations well.
_____have the position of "somebody" in the group.
_____do things without feeling that they are morally wrong.

People in this environment...

_____do things alone.
_____have the position of "somebody" in the group.
_____do things for other people.
_____have group leaders who back them up.
_____make decisions on their own.

People in this environment...

_____try out their own ideas.
_____receive recognition for the things they do.
_____have something different to do every day.
_____do things alone.
_____have assurance of continuing participation.

People in this environment...

_____have opportunities for self-advancement.
_____make use of their individual abilities.
_____receive recognition for the things they do.
_____make decisions on their own.
_____have group leaders who communicate expectations well.

People in this environment...

_____have good operating conditions.
_____do things alone.
_____have norms and practices that are observed consistently.
_____have opportunities for self advancement.
_____do things without feeling that they are morally wrong.

Please rank the five statements in each group on the basis of how well they describe the
environment mentioned on the front page. Write a "1" by the statement that best describes
the environment; write a "2" by the statement that provides the next best description;
continue ranking all five statements, using a "5" for the statement that describes the
environment least well.

People in this environment...
_____have the position of "somebody" in the group.
_____have good operating conditions.
_____are busy all the time.
_____get a feeling of accomplishment.
_____receive recognition for the things they do.

On the rest of this page we are asking you to do something different. This time, consider
each statement individually and decide whether or not it describes the environment.

--If you think that the statement describes the environment, circle "yes".

--If you think that the statement does not describe the environment, circle "No"

People in this environment...

1. make use of their individual abilities......................................Yes   No
2. get a feeling of accomplishment...Yes   No
3. are busy all the time..Yes   No
4. have opportunities for self-advancement....................................Yes   No
5. tell other people what to do...Yes   No
6. have norms and practices that are observed consistently....................Yes   No
7. are rewarded well in comparison with others................................Yes   No
8. are easy to make friends with..Yes   No
9. try out their own ideas..Yes   No
10. do things alone...Yes   No
11. do things without feeling that they are morally wrong.....................Yes   No
12. receive recognition for the things they do................................Yes   No
13. make decisions on their own...Yes   No
14. have assurance of continuing participation................................Yes   No
15. do things for other people..Yes   No
16. have the position of "somebody" in the group..............................Yes   No
17. have group leaders who back them up.......................................Yes   No
18. have group leaders who communicate expectations well......................Yes   No
19. have something different to do every day..................................Yes   No
20. have good operating conditions..Yes   No
21. plan their activities with little supervision.............................Yes   No

MINNESOTA SATISFACTION QUESTIONNAIRE-G

The purpose of this questionnaire is to give you a chance to tell how you feel about your present situation, what things you are satisfied with and what things you are not satisfied with.

On the next page you will find statements about your present situation.

- Read each statement carefully.

- Decide how satisfied you feel about the aspect of your situation described by the statement.

  Keeping the statement in mind:

        -if you feel that you are getting more than you expected, check the box under "Very Sat." (Very Satisfied);

        -if you feel that you are getting what you expected, check the box under "Sat." (Satisfied);

        -if you cannot make up your mind whether or not you are getting what you expected, check the box under "N" (Neither Satisfied nor Dissatisfied);

        -if you feel that you are getting less than you expected, check the box under "Dissat." (Dissatisfied);

        -if you feel that you are getting much less than you expected, check the box under "Very Dissat." (Very Dissatisfied).

- Remember: Keep the statement in mind when deciding how satisfied you feel about that aspect of your situation.

- Do this for all statements. Please answer every item.

Be frank and honest. Give a true picture of your feelings about your present situation.

Ask yourself: How satisfied am I with this aspect of my situation?

Very Sat. means I am very satisfied with this aspect.
Sat. means I am satisfied with this aspect.
N means I can't decide whether I am satisfied or not with this aspect.
Dissat. means I am dissatisfied with this aspect.
Very Dissat. means I am very dissatisfied with this aspect.

In my present situation, this is how I feel about..	Very Dissat.	Dissat.	N	Sat.	Very Sat.
1. Being able to stay busy...	—	—	—	—	—
2. The chance to be alone..	—	—	—	—	—
3. The chance to do something different every day..................	—	—	—	—	—
4. The chance to be "somebody" in the group........................	—	—	—	—	—
5. The way my group leader backs me up.............................	—	—	—	—	—
6. The way expectations are communicated by the group leader.......	—	—	—	—	—
7. Being able to do things without feeling they are morally wrong..	—	—	—	—	—
8. The way the group provides for my continuing participation......	—	—	—	—	—
9. The chance to do things for other people........................	—	—	—	—	—
10. The chance to tell people what to do...........................	—	—	—	—	—
11. The chance to make use of my best abilities....................	—	—	—	—	—
12. The way norms and practices are observed.......................	—	—	—	—	—
13. How my rewards compare with those of others....................	—	—	—	—	—
14. The chances for self-advancement...............................	—	—	—	—	—
15. The chance to make decisions on my own.........................	—	—	—	—	—
16. The chance to try out some of my own ideas.....................	—	—	—	—	—
17. The physical or operating conditions...........................	—	—	—	—	—
18. The friendliness of people in my group.........................	—	—	—	—	—
19. The recognition I get for the things I do......................	—	—	—	—	—
20. The feeling of accomplishment I get............................	—	—	—	—	—

MINNESOTA SATISFACTORINESS SCALES-G

Name_____Environment_____

Rated By_____Date_____

Please check the best answer for each question.
Be sure to answer all questions.

Compared with others in the group, how well does this person...	not as well	about the same	better
1. Observe norms and practices?...........................	___	___	___
2. Accept the direction of the group leader?.............	___	___	___
3. Follow standard rules and procedures?.................	___	___	___
4. Accept responsibility?................................	___	___	___
5. Adapt to changes in procedures or methods?...........	___	___	___
6. Respect the authority of the group leader?...........	___	___	___
7. Function as a member of a team?	___	___	
8. Get along with the group leader?.....................	___	___	___
9. Perform in routine situations?.......................	___	___	___
10. Get along with others?..............................	___	___	___
11. Perform in situations requiring variety and change....	___	___	___

Compared with others in the group...	not as good	about the same	better
12. How good is the quality of his/her performance?.......	___	___	___
13. How good is the quantity of his/her performance?......	___	___	___

If you could make the decision, would you...	yes	not sure	no
14. Give him/her some reward or recognition?..............	___	___	___
15. Give him/her a position at a higher level?............	___	___	___
16. Give him/her a position of more responsibility?.......	___	___	___

Please check the best answer for each question
Be sure to answer all questions

Compared with others in the group, how often does this person...	less	about the same	more
17. Come late for appointments?	___	___	___
18. Become overexcited?	___	___	___
19. Become upset and unhappy?	___	___	___
20. Need disciplinary action?	___	___	___
21. Stay absent from meetings?	___	___	___
22. Seem bothered by something?	___	___	___
23. Complain about physical ailments?	___	___	___
24. Say 'odd' things?	___	___	___
25. Seem to tire easily?	___	___	___
26. Act as if he/she is not listening when spoken to?	___	___	___
27. Wander from subject to subject when talking?	___	___	___

28. Now will you please consider this person with respect to overall competence, effectiveness of performance, proficiency, and general overall value. Take into account all the elements of successful performance, such as knowledge of duties and functions to be performed, quantity and quality of output, relations with other people (subordinates, equals, superiors), ability to get things done, intelligence, interest, response to training, and the like. In other words, how closely does he/she approximate the ideal, the kind of person you want more of? With all these factors in mind, where would you rank this person as compared with the other people whom you now have in the same capacity? (or, if he/she is the only one, how does he/she compare with those who have been in this same capacity?)

In the top 1/4...___

In the top half but not among the top 1/4...............................___

In the bottom half but not among the lowest 1/4.........................___

In the lowest 1/4...___

C /IS   TAXON: 611

Primary Taxon: 42   Level code: 020.220

OCCUPATIONAL REQUIREMENTS

DOT Title	Perceptual Abilities S, P, Q NOT SIGNIF		Cognitive Abilities G, V, N HIGH		Motor Abilities K, F, M NOT SIGNIF		
	DOT Code GRP / DPT / EC	DOT Profile INT / TMP / PHY	Job Des DOT / OOH	Additional Data FX / PR / OAP / SCH / ORP / ORC / INV			

OCCUPATIONAL REINFORCERS

DOT Title	GRP	DPT	EC	INT	TMP	PHY	DOT	OOH	FX	PR	OAP	SCH	ORP	ORC	INV
CLERGY MEMBER — minister, preacher, priest, rabbi	120	007	010	465 8	594 56	SL4	D77	119	HI	HI	49	VR	YES	A	SK
COUNSELOR — guidance counselor, school counselor, vocational advisor, vocational counselor	045	107	010	465 8	594 56	SL4	D48	134	HI	HI	49	VR	YES	A	K
DIRECTOR, RELIGIOUS EDUCATION	129	107	022	465 8	594 56	SL4	D77	119	HI	HI	53	VR	NO	A	K
GROUP WORKER	195	164	010	465 8	594 56	L6	144	000	MI	MI	00	VR	NO		
PSYCHOLOGIST, COUNSELING	045	107	026	465 8	594 56	SL4	D49	104	HI	HI	49	VR	YES	A	SK
PSYCHOLOGIST, CLINICAL	045	107	022	465 8	594 56	SL4	D49	104	HI	HI	49	VR	YES	A	SK
PSYCHOLOGIST, SCHOOL	045	107	034	465 8	594 56	SL4	D49	104	HI	HI	49	VR	YES	A	SK
SOCIAL GROUP WORKER	195	107	022	465 8	594 56	SL4	144	000	HI	HI	00	VR	NO		SK

GRP--DOT (1977) Occupational Group (3-digit code)
DPT--DOT (1977) Worker-Function Code for data, people, things
EC---DOT (1977) extended code (last three digits)
INT--Interests (DOT, Vol. II. Occupational Classificaton--third edition 1965)
TMP--Temperaments (DOT, Vol. II., Occupational Classification--third edition 1965)
PHY--Physical Demands (DOT, Vol. II., Occupational Classification--third edition 1965)
DOT--Page number for Occupational Description in the DOT (1977)
OOH--Page number in the Occupational Outlook Handbook (1986-1987)
FX---Estimated Flexibility of the Work Environment
PR---Occupational Prestige Level
OAP--Occupational Aptitude Pattern (where available)
SCH--Schedule of Reinforcement
ORP--Availability of Occupational Reinforcer Pattern
ORC--Occupational Reinforcer Cluster (where available)
INV--Interest Inventory Containing Occupational Scale (where available)

GRP - DOT (First 3 digits) - General category of work related activities
DPT - DOT (Second 3 digits) - Worker functions

Data (4th digit)	**People** (5th digit)	**Things** (6th Digit)
0 Synthesizing	0 Mentoring	0 Setting-up
1 Coordinating	1 Negotiating	1 Precision Working
2 Analyzing	2 Instructing	2 Operating - Controlling
3 Compiling	3 Supervising	3 Driving - Operating
4 Computing	4 Diverting	4 Manipulating
5 Copying	5 Persuading	5 Tending
6 Comparing	6 Speaking - Signaling	6 Feeding - Offbearing
	7 Serving	7 Handling
	8 Taking Instructions - Helping	

INT - Situations involving a preference for work activities *(see Appendix K):*

1. Dealing with things and objects	vs.	6. Concerned with people and communication of ideas
2. Involving business contact with people	vs.	7. Of a scientific and technical nature
3. Of a routine, concrete organized nature	vs.	8. Of an abstract and creative nature
4. Working with people for their presumed good	vs.	9. Nonsocial, carried out in relation to processes, machines and techniques
5. Resulting in prestige or esteem of others	vs.	0. Resulting in tangible, productive satisfaction

TMP - Types of occupational situations to which workers must adjust *(see Appendix L):*
1. Variety of duties characterized by frequent change
2. Repetitive or short cycle operations carried out to set procedures
3. Following specific instruction with little independent action or judgment
4. Direction, control, planning of entire activity or the activity of others
5. Dealing with people beyond the giving and receiving of instructions
6. Working alone, physically isolated
7. Influencing others in their opinions, attitudes or judgments
8. Performing adequately under stress
9. Evaluation of information against sensory or judgmental criteria
0. Evaluation of information against measurable or verifiable criteria
X. Interpretation of feelings, ideas, or facts in terms of personal viewpoint
Y. Precise attainment of set limits, tolerances or standards

PHY - Physical demands required of a worker on the job *(see Appendix M):*
S = Sedentary work (max 10 lbs. - little walking or standing)
L = Light work (max 20 lbs.)
M = Medium work (max 50 lbs.)
H = Heavy work (max 100 lbs.)
V = Very heavy work (max greater than 100 lbs.)

2 = Climbing and/or balancing
3 = Stooping, kneeling, crouching, and/or crawling
4 = Reaching, handling, fingering, and/or feeling
5 = Talking and/or hearing
6 = Seeing

FX - Index of amount of deviation of worker capabilities from job requirements that will be tolerated by the work environment *(see Appendix D):*
LOW = Worker capabilities must match job requirements closely
MOD = Worker capabilities can vary somewhat from job requirements
HI = Worker capabilities can vary significantly from job requirements

PR - Index of the amount of prestige associated with occupations *(see Appendix E):*
AV = Average prestige
MOD = Moderate prestige
MH = Moderately high prestige
HI = High prestige

SCH - Estimates of occupational reinforcement delivery schedules *(see Appendix F):*

F = Fixed	V = Variable	R = Ratio	I = Interval

INV - Interest Inventories where Occupational Scale is Available:
K = Kuder Occupational Interest Survey
S = Strong-Campbell Interest Inventory

Minnesota Ability Rating Scale (MARS)

1.   In this questionnaire we would like you to estimate your abilities.

2.   On the following pages you will find statements about different kinds of abilities. Please read each statement carefully.

3.   Ask yourself: How much of the ability described in each statement do I have?

4.   Next to the statement are the numbers 1 through 6.

5.   Circle the highest number that you think best describes your ability.

   Circle "1" if you think you are in the bottom 10%
     of the population (the bottom 1 of every 10)

   Circle "2" if you think you are in the bottom 33%
     of the population (the bottom 1 in every 3)

   Circle "3" if you think you are average (the middle 1 in every 3)

   Circle "4" if you think you are as good as the top 33%
     of the population (the best 1 in every 3)

   Circle "5" if you think you are as good as the top 10%
     of the population (the best 1 in every 10)

   Circle "6" if you think you are as good as the top 1%
     of the population (the best 1 in every 100)

6.   Please do this for all the statements on the following pages.

7.   Do not turn back to previous statements.

How much ability do you have to:	Circle a number for each statement					
	Bottom 10%	Bottom 33%	Mid. 33%	Top 33%	Top 10%	Top 1%
1. Use hands and arms to handle objects quickly and correctly	1	2	3	4	5	6
2. Do number problems quickly and accurately	1	2	3	4	5	6
3. Pick out similar objects in a group	1	2	3	4	5	6
4. Think about a problem and decide the best way to solve it	1	2	3	4	5	6
5. Pick out errors in written material or lists of names quickly	1	2	3	4	5	6
6. Know if words have the same or opposite meanings	1	2	3	4	5	6
7. Put together small objects quickly	1	2	3	4	5	6
8. Know how an object would look based on a drawing of it	1	2	3	4	5	6
9. Move fingers rapidly and accurately in using machines	1	2	3	4	5	6
10. Understand ideas written in books or manuals	1	2	3	4	5	6
11. Use very small tools to put together or fix things	1	2	3	4	5	6
12. Pick out objects that have the same shape even if the color and shading are different	1	2	3	4	5	6
13. Position heavy objects accurately	1	2	3	4	5	6
14. Know quickly if words or names are the same	1	2	3	4	5	6
15. Solve problems using words, numbers and drawings	1	2	3	4	5	6
16. Write down or code information quickly and correctly	1	2	3	4	5	6
17. Use simple arithmetic to solve problems	1	2	3	4	5	6

How much ability do you have to:	Circle a number for each statement					
	Bottom 10%	Bottom 33%	Mid. 33%	Top 33%	Top 10%	Top 1%
18. See how objects with different shapes fit together	1	2	3	4	5	6
19. Understand written words and ideas	1	2	3	4	5	6
20. Use fingers quickly to put together or take apart small objects	1	2	3	4	5	6
21. Work with both objects and ideas	1	2	3	4	5	6
22. Pick things up and put them in place quickly	1	2	3	4	5	6
23. See how objects and drawings are the same or different	1	2	3	4	5	6
24. Solve problems by adding, subtracting, multiplying or dividing	1	2	3	4	5	6
25. Fill in forms quickly and correctly	1	2	3	4	5	6
26. Find small differences between printed words quickly	1	2	3	4	5	6
27. See how the parts of an object fit together to form the object	1	2	3	4	5	6
28. Use hands to pick up objects quickly and put them in place correctly	1	2	3	4	5	6
29. Match objects by their shape and shading	1	2	3	4	5	6
30. Use eyes and hands together quickly and correctly	1	2	3	4	5	6
31. Know the meanings of words	1	2	3	4	5	6
32. Put together or take apart small objects with the fingers	1	2	3	4	5	6
33. Use numbers, words and figures in making decisions	1	2	3	4	5	6
34. Pick out mistakes in sentences or lists of names quickly	1	2	3	4	5	6

How much ability do you have to:		Circle a number for each statement					
		Bottom 10%	Bottom 33%	Mid. 33%	Top 33%	Top 10%	Top 1%
35.	Solve on-the-job problems requiring adding, subtracting, multiplying or dividing	1	2	3	4	5	6
36.	See what an object would look like if its shape changes	1	2	3	4	5	6
37.	Understand ideas suggested by words	1	2	3	4	5	6
38.	Make quick, correct moves with the hands and fingers	1	2	3	4	5	6
39.	Work with numbers quickly and accurately	1	2	3	4	5	6
40.	Place small objects in a definite spot quickly and correctly	1	2	3	4	5	6
41.	Tell how objects that look alike are really different	1	2	3	4	5	6
42.	Pick out important deetails in written words or names quickly	1	2	3	4	5	6
43.	Understand instructions and what they mean	1	2	3	4	5	6
44.	Pick up objects and put them in a definite place quickly	1	2	3	4	5	6
45.	Know how an object would look from a drawing of it	1	2	3	4	5	6

Scoring Guide for the MARS

Directions:
1. Enter ratings from questionnaire for the appropriate item in the column Rating.
2. Copy the ratings from the column Rating onto the columns G, V, N, etc. as indicated.
3. Add the ratings down the columns G, V, N, etc and enter in row Total.
4. Compute averages by dividing column totals by 5.

Item	Rating	G	V	N	S	P	Q	K	F	M
1. M	___									1.___
2. N	___			2.___						
3. P	___					3.___				
4. G	___	4.___								
5. Q	___						5.___			
6. V	___		6.___							
7. F	___								7.___	
8. S	___				8.___					
9. K	___							9.___		
10. V	___		10.___							
11. F	___								11.___	
12. P	___					12.___				
13. M	___									13.___
14. Q	___						14.___			
15. G	___	15.___								
16. V	___							16.___		
17. N	___			17.___						
18. S	___				18.___					
19. V	___		19.___							
20. F	___								20.___	
21. G	___	21.___								
22. M	___									22.___
23. P	___					23.___				
24. N	___			24.___						
25. K	___							25.___		
26. Q	___						26.___			
27. S	___				27.___					
28. M	___									28.___
29. P	___					29.___				
30. K	___							30.___		
31. V	___		31.___							
32. F	___								32.___	
33. G	___	33.___								
34. Q	___						34.___			
35. N	___			35.___						
36. S	___				36.___					
37. V	___		37.___							
38. K	___							38.___		
39. N	___			39.___						
40. F	___								40.___	
41. P	___					41.___				
42. Q	___						42.___			
43. G	___	43.___								
44. M	___									44.___
45. S	___				45.___					
Totals		‾G‾	‾V‾	‾N‾	‾S‾	‾P‾	‾Q‾	‾K‾	‾F‾	‾M‾
Average		___	___	___	___	___	___	___	___	___

Minnesota Ability Requirement Rating Scale (MARRS)

1. We would like you to estimate the abilities required in the target environment. The environment we are concerned with is:_____.

2. On the following pages you will find statements about different kinds of abilities. read each statement carefully.

3. Ask yourself: How much of the ability described in each statement is required?

4. Next to the statement are the numbers 1 through 6.

5. Circle the highest number that you think best describes the ability level required.

   Circle "1" if you think the level required is the bottom 10% of the population (the bottom 1 of every 10)

   Circle "2" if you think the level required is the bottom 33% of the population (the bottom 1 in every 3)

   Circle "3" if you think average ability is required (the middle 1 in every 3)

   Circle "4" if you think the level required is the top 33% of the population (the best 1 in every 3)

   Circle "5" if you think the level required is the top 10% of the population (the best 1 in every 10)

   Circle "6" if you think the level required is the top 1% of the population (the best 1 in every 100)

6. Please do this for all the statements on the following pages.

7. Do not turn back to previous statements.

How much of this ability is required in the target environment:	Circle a number for each statement					
	Bottom 10%	Bottom 33%	Mid. 33%	Top 33%	Top 10%	Top 1%
1. Using hands and arms to handle objects quickly and correctly	1	2	3	4	5	6
2. Doing number problems quickly and accurately	1	2	3	4	5	6
3. Picking out similar objects in a group	1	2	3	4	5	6
4. Thinking about a problem and decide the best way to solve it	1	2	3	4	5	6
5. Picking out errors in written material or lists of names quickly	1	2	3	4	5	6
6. Knowing if words have the same or opposite meanings	1	2	3	4	5	6
7. Putting together small objects quickly	1	2	3	4	5	6
8. Knowing how an object would look based on a drawing of it	1	2	3	4	5	6
9. Moving fingers rapidly and accurately in using machine	1	2	3	4	5	6
10. Understanding ideas written in books or manuals	1	2	3	4	5	6
11. Using very small tools to put together or fix things	1	2	3	4	5	6
12. Picking out objects that have the same shape even if the color and shading are different	1	2	3	4	5	6
13. Positioning heavy objects accurately	1	2	3	4	5	6
14. Knowing quickly if words or names are the same	1	2	3	4	5	6
15. Solving problems using words, numbers and drawings	1	2	3	4	5	6
16. Writing down or coding information quickly and correctly	1	2	3	4	5	6
17. Using simple arithmetic to solve problems	1	2	3	4	5	6

How much of this ability is required in the target environment:	Circle a number for each statement					
	Bottom 10%	Bottom 33%	Mid. 33%	Top 33%	Top 10%	Top 10%
18. Seeing how objects with different shapes fit together	1	2	3	4	5	6
19. Understanding written words and ideas	1	2	3	4	5	6
20. Using fingers quickly to put together or take apart small objects	1	2	3	4	5	6
21. Working with both objects and ideas	1	2	3	4	5	6
22. Picking things up and put them in place quickly	1	2	3	4	5	6
23. Seeing how objects and drawings are the same or different	1	2	3	4	5	6
24. Solving problems by adding, subtracting, multiplying or dividing	1	2	3	4	5	6
25. Filling in forms quickly and correctly	1	2	3	4	5	6
26. Finding small differences between printed words quickly	1	2	3	4	5	6
27. Seeing how the parts of an object fit together to form the object	1	2	3	4	5	6
28. Using hands to pick up objects quickly and putting them in place correctly	1	2	3	4	5	6
29. Matching objects by their shape and shading	1	2	3	4	5	6
30. Using eyes and hands together quickly and correctly	1	2	3	4	5	6
31. Knowing the meanings of words	1	2	3	4	5	6
32. Putting together or taking apart small objects with the fingers	1	2	3	4	5	6
33. Using numbers, words and figures in making decisions	1	2	3	4	5	6
34. Picking out mistakes in sentences or lists of names quickly	1	2	3	4	5	6

How much of this ability is required in the target environment:		Circle a number for each statement					
		Bottom 10%	Bottom 33%	Mid. 33%	Top 33%	Top 10%	Top 10%
35.	Solving on-the-job problems requiring adding, subtracting, multiplying or dividing	1	2	3	4	5	6
36.	Seeing what an object would look like if its shape changes	1	2	3	4	5	6
37.	Understanding ideas suggested by words	1	2	3	4	5	6
38.	Making quick, correct moves with the hands and fingers	1	2	3	4	5	6
39.	Working with numbers quickly and accurately	1	2	3	4	5	6
40.	Placing small objects in a definite spot quickly and correctly	1	2	3	4	5	6
41.	Telling how objects that look alike are really different	1	2	3	4	5	6
42.	Picking out important deetails in written words or names quickly	1	2	3	4	5	6
43.	Understanding instructions and what they mean	1	2	3	4	5	6
44.	Picking up objects and puttin them in a definite place quickly	1	2	3	4	5	6
45.	Knowing how an object would look from a drawing of it	1	2	3	4	5	6

MINNESOTA ADJUSTMENT STYLE CHECKLIST (MASC)

On the basis of biographical information, interview data, and counselor inference, this client is likely to:

_____1.   Generate social events

_____2.   Be a jogger

_____3.   Never break school rules

_____4.   Write letters to the editor

_____5.   Endure a dissatisfying job

_____6.   Leave a dull social situation

_____7.   Quit school

_____8.   Leave part of a job undone

_____9.   Wait for social events to occur

____10.   Join a conversation group

____11.   Be a political liberal

____12.   Join Toastmasters

____13.   Quit a job

____14.   Opt for loose structuring of rules

____15.   Ask for a raise

____16.   Adhere strictly to established traditions

____17.   Vote against a strike

____18.   Join a professional association

____19.   Adapt to a cultural change

____20.   Advocate more rules and laws

____21.   Join a church group

____22.   Promote a work slowdown

____23.   See a marriage counselor

____24.   Join a militant organization

___25.   Join a veterans group

___26.   Be a political conservative

___27.   Promote a strike

___28.   Endure an uninteresting social event

___29.   Cheat in school for grades

___30.   Find a way to do unpleasant parts of a job

___31.   Ask for a divorce

___32   Refuse to participate in a work slowdown

___33.   Be a political independent

___34.   Ask for a marriage separation

___35.   Participate in public protest demonstrations

___36.   Adapt to school because it is expected

___37.   Continue a stormy marriage

___38.   Work harder for a raise

___39.   Hope that time will improve a marriage

___40.   Ask for a transfer to other duties

___41.   Join an exercise of fitness club

___42.   Learn skills beyond those required by duties

___43.   Take action to change an environment

___44.   Work to improve vocabulary

___45.   Tolerate dissatisfying situations

___46.   Be a born-again Christian

___47.   Work hard to present a pleasant personality

Would you describe this person as:

___48.	Open		___68.	Amenable
___49.	Aggressive		___67.	Contentious
___50.	Reactive		___69.	Resilient
___51.	Rigid		___70.	Inflexible
___52.	Active		___71.	Forceful
___53.	Quiet		___72.	Subdued
___54.	Manipulative		___73.	Contriving
___55.	Flexible		___74.	Pliable
___56.	Passive		___75.	Unassertive
___57.	Helpful		___76.	Supportive
___58.	Accommodating		___77.	Adaptable
___59.	Receptive		___78.	Open-minded
___60.	Self-aggrandizing		___79.	Braggart
___61.	Closed		___80.	Stolid
___62.	Self-effacing		___81.	Withdrawn
___63.	Flamboyant		___82.	Ostentatious
___64.	Guarded		___83.	Cautious
___65.	Pushy		___84.	Obnoxious
___66.	Reserved		___85.	Restrained
___67.	Timid		___86.	Fearful

Key: A = Active, R = Reactive, F = Flexible, I = Inflexible. Infer style likelihood from ratios of Active to Reactive, and Reactive plus Flexible to Inflexible.

1-A; 2-R; 3-I; 4-A; 5-F; 6-A; 7-A; 8-A; 9-F; 10-A,I; 11-A; 12-R; 13-A; 14-F; 15-A; 16-I; 17I; 18-R; F-19; 20-I; 21-R; 22-A; 23-R; 24-A; 25-A,I; 26-A,I; 27-A; 28-F; 29-A; 30-F; 31-A; 32-I; 33-A; 34-A; 35-A; 36-F; 37-F; 38-R; 39-F; 40-A; 41-R; 42-R; 43-A; 44-R; 45-F; 46-I; 47-R; 48-F; 49-A; 50-R; 51-I; 52-A; 53-Q; 54-A; 55-F; 56-F; 57-A; 58-F,R; 59-F; 60-A; 61-I; 62-R,F; 63-A; 64-I; 65-I; 66-A; 67-I; 68-R; 69-F; 70-A; 71-F; 72-I; 73-A; 74-R; 75-A; 76-F; 77-F; 78-A; 79-F,R; 80-F; 81-A; 82-I; 83-R; 84-A; 85-I; 86-I; 87-A,I; 88-I; 89-R

MINNESOTA NEED ESTIMATION SCALE (MNES)

The following is a list of the needs measured by the Minnesota Importance
Questionnaire. Rank the needs in the order of importance to you. Assign number 1
to the need most important to you. Then assign number 20 to the need least
important to you. Follow this with number 2 to the need that is second most
important to you. Then number 19 to the need that is second least important. Continue
this alternate ranking procedure until all needs have been ranked.

Rank

_____ 1.   ABILITY UTILIZATION: I could do something that makes use of
            my abilities.

_____ 2.   ACHIEVEMENT: I could get a feeling of accomplishment.

_____ 3.   ACTIVITY: I could be busy all the time.

_____ 4.   ADVANCEMENT: I could have an opportunity for self-advancement.

_____ 5.   AUTHORITY: I could tell people what to do.

_____ 6.   CO-GROUP MEMBERS: People in my group would be easy to make
            friends with.

_____ 7.   COMPENSATION: My rewards compare well with those of others.

       8.   CREATIVITY: I could try out my own ideas.

_____ 9.   INDEPENDENCE: I could be alone.

_____10.   LEADERSHIP--HUMAN RELATIONS: My group leader would back me up.

_____11.   LEADERSHIP--TECHNICAL: My group leader would communicate
           expectations well.

_____12.   MORAL VALUES: I could do things without feeling they are morally wrong.

_____13.   NORMS AND PRACTICES: Norms and practices are observed consistently.

_____14.   OPERATING CONDITIONS: I could have good operating conditions.

_____15.   RECOGNITION: I could get recognition for the things I do.

_____16.   RESPONSIBILITY: I could make decisions on my own.

_____17.   SECURITY: The group would provide for my continuing participation.

_____18.   SOCIAL SERVICE: I could do things for other people.

_____19.   SOCIAL STATUS: I could be "somebody" in the group.

_____20.   VARIETY: I could do something different every day.

References

Anastasi, A. (1958). *Differential psychology* (3rd ed.). New York: Macmillan.

Anderson, L. M. (1969). *Longitudinal changes in level of work adjustment*. Unpublished doctoral dissertation, University of Minnesota.

Bergmark, R. E. (1988). *A systematic examination of determinants and correlates of vocational needs as measured by the Minnesota Importance Questionnaire*. Unpublished doctoral dissertation, University of Minnesota.

Betz, E. L. (1969). Need reinforcer correspondence as a predictor of job satisfaction. *Personnel and Guidance Journal, 47*, 878-883.

Borgen, F. H., Weiss, D. J., Tinsley, H. E. A., Dawis, R. V., & Lofquist, L. H. (1968). *Occupational reinforcer patterns* (Minnesota Studies in Vocational Rehabilitation XXIV). Minneapolis: Industrial Relations Center, University of Minnesota.

Cannon, W. B. (1932). *The wisdom of the body*. New York: Norton.

Carlson, R. E., Dawis, R. V., England, G. W., & Lofquist, L. H. (1963). *The measurement of employment satisfactoriness* (Minnesota Studies in Vocational Rehabilitation XIV). Minneapolis: Industrial Relations Center, University of Minnesota.

Carlson, R.E., Dawis, R. V., & Weiss, D. J. (1969). The effect of satisfaction on the relationship between abilities and satisfactoriness. *Occupational Psychology, 43*, 39–46.

Chartrand, J. M. (1988). *The effect of multiple role participation on the personal and academic adjustment of students*. Unpublished doctoral dissertation, University of Minnesota.

Cheung, F. M. (1975). *A threshold model of flexibility as a personality style dimension in work adjustment*. Unpublished doctoral dissertation, University of Minnesota.

Dawis, R. V., Dohm, T. E., Lofquist, L. H., Chartrand, J. M., & Due, A. M. (1987). *Minnesota Occupational Classification System III*. Minneapolis: Vocational Psychology Research, Department of Psychology, University of Minnesota.

Dawis, R. V., & Lofquist, L. H. (1984). *A psychological theory of work adjustment*. Minneapolis: University of Minnesota Press.

Dvorak, B. J. (1935). Differential occupational ability patterns. *Bulletin of the Employment Stabilization Research Institute, 3*, 3.

Ellis, A. (1962). *Reason and emotion in psychotherapy*. New York: Lyle Stuart.

Freud, S. (1943). *A general introduction to psychoanalysis* (J. Riviere, trans.). New York: Garden City.

Gay, E. G., Weiss, D. J., Hendel, D. D., Dawis, R. V., & Lofquist, L. H. (1971). *Manual for the Minnesota Importance Questionnaire* (Minnesota Studies in Vocational Rehabilitation XXVIII). Minneapolis: Industrial Relations Center, University of Minnesota.

Ghiselli, E. E. (1966). *The validity of occupational aptitude tests*. New York: Wiley.

Gibson, D. L., Weiss, D. J., Dawis, R. V., & Lofquist, L. H. (1970). *Manual for the Minnesota Satisfactoriness Scales* (Minnesota Studies in Vocational Rehabilitation XVIII). Minneapolis: Industrial Relations Center, University of Minnesota.

Hansen, J. C., & Campbell, D. P. (1985). *Manual for the SVIB-SCII*. Palo Alto, Calif.: Consulting Psychologists Press.

Holland, J. L. (1973). *Making vocational choices: A theory of careers*. Englewood Cliffs, N. J.: Prentice-Hall.

Humphrey, C. C. (1980). *A multitrait-multimethod assessment of personality styles in work adjustment*. Unpublished doctoral dissertation, University of Minnesota.

Kuder, G. F. (1977). *Activity interests and occupational choice*. Chicago: Science Research Associates.

Lofquist, L. H., Siess, T. F., Dawis, R. V., England, G. W., & Weiss, D. J. (1964). *Disability and work* (Minnesota Studies in Vocational Rehabilitation XVII). Minneapolis: Industrial Relations Center, University of Minnesota.

Minton, H. L., & Schneider, F. W. (1980). *Differential psychology*. Monterey, Calif.: Brooks/Cole.

Murray, H. A. (1938). *Explorations in personality*. New York: Oxford University Press.

Parsons, F. (1909). *Choosing a vocation*. Boston: Houghton Mifflin.

Paterson, D. G. (1930). *Physique and intellect*. New York: Century.

Paterson, D. G., Gerken, C. d'A., & Hahn, M. E. (1953). *Revised Minnesota Occupational Rating Scales*. Minneapolis: University of Minnesota Press.

Roe, A. (1956). *The psychology of occupations*. New York: Wiley.

Rogers, C. R. (1951). *Client-centered therapy*. Boston: Houghton Mifflin.

Rosen, S. D., Weiss, D. J., Hendel, D. D., Dawis, R. V., & Lofquist, L. H. (1972). *Occupational reinforcer patterns* (Vol. 2). (Minnesota Studies in Vocational Rehabilitation XXIX). Minneapolis: Industrial Relations Center, University of Minnesota.

Rounds, J. B., Jr. (1981). *The comparative and combined utility of need and interest data in the prediction of job satisfaction*. Unpublished doctoral dissertation, University of Minnesota.

Rounds, J. B., Jr., Dawis, R. V., & Lofquist, L. H. (1979). Life history correlates of vocational needs for a female adult sample. *Journal of Counseling Psychology, 26*, 487-496.

Rounds, J. B., Jr., Henly, G. A., Dawis, R. V., Lofquist, L. H., & Weiss, D. J. (1981). *Manual for the Minnesota Importance Questionnaire: A measure of vocational needs and values*. Minneapolis: Department of Psychology, University of Minnesota.

Selye, H. (1946). The general adaptation syndrome and the diseases of adaptation. *Journal of Clinical Endocrinology, 6*, 117-230.

Skinner, B. F. (1938). *The behavior of organisms*. New York: Appleton-Century-Crofts.

Strong, E. K., Jr. (1943). *Vocational interests of men and women*. Stanford, Calif.: Stanford University Press.

Strong, E. K., Jr. (1955). *Vocational interests 18 years after college*. Minneapolis: University of Minnesota Press.

Super, D. E. (1957). *The psychology of careers*. New York: Harper & Row.

Super, D. E. (1962). The structure of work values in relation to status, achievement, interests, and adjustment. *Journal of Applied Psychology, 42*, 231-239.

Tyler, L. E. (1965). *The psychology of individual differences* (3rd ed.). New York: Appleton-Century-Crofts.

U.S. Department of Labor. (1970). *Manual for the USES General Aptitude Test Battery*. Washington, D.C.: U.S. Government Printing Office.

U.S. Department of Labor. (1977). *Dictionary of occupational titles* (4th ed.). Washington, D.C.: U.S. Government Printing Office.

U.S. Department of Labor. (1979). *Manual for the USES General Aptitude Test Battery, Section II: Occupational aptitude pattern structure*. Washington, D.C.: U.S. Government Printing Office.

Viteles, M. S. (1932). *Industrial psychology*. New York: Norton.

Weiss, D. J., Dawis, R. V., England, G. W., & Lofquist, L. H. (1967). *Manual for the Minnesota Satisfaction Questionnaire* (Minnesota Studies in Vocational Rehabilitation XXII). Minneapolis: Industrial Relations Center, University of Minnesota.

Willerman, L. (1979). *The psychology of individual and group differences*. San Francisco: Freeman.

Williams, R. G. (1956). *Biochemical individuality, the basis for the genotrophic concept*. New York: Wiley.

Index

Abilities, 22, 23; content areas, 40; origin of, 39; process areas, 40
Activeness, 18, 23
Addiction counseling, 98
Adjustment, 23; modes, 18, 23; origin of, 42; style, 17, 23
Anastasi, A., 5, 36
Anderson, L. M., 37
Applications: and P-E-C Theory, 86ff.
Assessment: approaches, 74; caveats, 76-77; validity and reliability, 75-76

Bergmark, R. E., 37
Betz, E. L., 37
Biographical Information Form (BIF), 78-80
Borgen, F. H., 36, 81

Campbell, D. P., 73
Cannon, W. B., 37
Career counseling, 87
Carlson, R. E., 37
Celerity, 16, 24
Chartrand, J. M., 38
Cheung, F. M., 38
Client behavior, 47, 50-52
Correspondence, 22, 24; perception of, 44-45
Corresponsiveness, 22, 24, 97
Counseling: behavior, 47, 54-61; for job change, 90; process, 46-50, 54-61; for self-esteem, 100

Dawis, R. V., 9, 12, 16, 87
Decline stage: and behavior development, 20, 23
Diagnostic hypotheses, 52-53

Dictionary of Occupational Titles (DOT), 11, 36
Differentiation stage: and behavior development, 20, 23
Dvorak, B., 11, 36, 37, 84

Educational curricula, planning, 104
Educational reinforcer patterns (ERPs), 104
Ellis, Albert, 9
Empiricism, dustbowl, ix
Employee morale, 103
Endurance, 17, 24
Environment "personality," 20
Environmental differences, 6

Family counseling, 92
Flexibility, 17, 24
Freud, S., 7

Gay, E. G., 80
General Aptitude Test Battery (GATB), 14, 84
Gerken, C. d'A., 8
Ghiselli, E. E., 11, 37
Gibson, D. L., 84

Hahn, M. E., 8
Hansen, J. C., 73
Holland, J., 11, 73
Homeostasis, 7, 37
Humphrey, C. C., 38

Individual differences, 3, 5-6, 24
Instrumentation: and P-E-C Theory, 78-85
Interests, 24-25, 72-73; origin of, 43

Job-adjustment counseling, 88

Job psychograph, 8
Job training programs, 104
Job transfer, 102

Kuder, G. F., 73

Lofquist, L. H., 9, 16, 87, 89

Marriage counseling, 91
Minnesota Ability Rating Scale (MARS), 85
Minnesota Ability Requirement Rating Scale (MARRS), 85
Minnesota Adjustment Style Checklist (MASC), 85
Minnesota Environment Description Questionnaire (MEDQ), 81
Minnesota Importance Questionnaire (MIQ), 11, 14, 80
Minnesota Job Description Questionnaire (MJDQ), 81
Minnesota Need Estimation Scale (MNES), 85
Minnesota Occupational Classification System III (MOCS III), 12, 21, 22, 84
Minnesota Point of View, ix
Minnesota Satisfaction Questionnaire (MSQ), 81
Minnesota Satisfactoriness Scales (MSS), 84
Minton, H. L., 5
Motivation, 18
Murray, H., 11

Needs, psychological, 1, 3, 25, 26, 28, 41

Occupational Ability/Aptitude Patterns (OAPs), 21
Occupational Reinforcer Patterns (ORPs), 21

Pace, 17, 25
Parsons, F., 7
Paterson, D. G., ix, 8, 11
P-E-C counseling, 3-4
Perseverance, 18, 25
Person-Environment-Correspondence (P-E-C) Theory, defined, 1
Personality, 13, 25; development, 18; structure, 13, 25-26

Personality style, 16, 26; origin of, 42
Personnel selection, 101
Preconditions: and counseling, 53-54
Presenting problems, 26; origin of, 44
Propositions: and P-E-C Theory, 29-33

Rational Emotive Therapy, 9
Reactiveness, 18, 26
Reference dimensions, 15
Reinforcement, 26
Reinforcer, 26-27
Research hypotheses: and P-E-C Theory, 33-35
Research questions, 107-8
Research supporting P-E-C Theory, 35-38
Responses, 27
Retirement counseling, 94
Rewards, 27
Rhythm, 17, 27
Roe, A., 8
Rogers, C., 9
Rosen, S. D., 36
Rounds, J. B., 9, 14, 37, 38, 80

Salary equity problems, 103
Salient importance environment, 27
Salient problem environment, 27
Satisfaction, 27
Satisfactoriness, 27
Schneider, F. W., 5
Self-image, 27, 44-45; accuracy, 63-64; assessment, 64-67; change, 67-71; definition, 62; importance, 63
Selye, H., 37
Skill, 27
Skinner, B. F., 10
Social norms, 28
Stability stage: and behavior development, 23
Stress counseling, 97
Strong, E. K., Jr., 11
Super, D., 10

Target environment, 28, 58-59
Teaching career courses, 105
Theory of Work Adjustment (TWA), 1
Tyler, L. E., 36

Unemployment counseling, 91

Values, 16, 28, 42; origin of, 41
Viteles, M., 8
Vocational rehabilitation counseling, 89

Weiss, D. J., x, 81

Willerman, L., 5
Williams, R. G., 5, 36
Work environments, design of, 102
Work Values Inventory (WVI), 10